*The Four Ordinary Foundations
of
Buddhist Practice*

Bibliotheca Indo-Buddhica Series No. 137

The Four Ordinary Foundations of Buddhist Practice
(Tib. *tün mong gi ngön dro shi*)

by

The Venerable
Khenchen Thrangu, Rinpoche
Abbot of Rumtek Monastery

Translated by
Ken and Katia Holmes

Sri Satguru Publications
A Division of
Indian Books Centre
Delhi, India

Published by:
SRI SATGURU PUBLICATIONS

Published by
Sri Satguru Publications
A Division of
Indian Books Centre
24/4, Shakti Nagar, Near Dena Bank, Delhi-110007

Copyright © 1990 by Namo Buddha Seminar, 1390 Kalmia Avenue, Boulder, CO 80304, U. S. A.

First Edition : Delhi, 1994
ISBN 81-7030-416-4

All rights reserved. No part of this book, either text or art, may be reproduced in any form, electronic or otherwise, without written permission from the Namo Buddha Seminar.

Acknowledgements

We would like to thank the many persons who helped make this book possible. First of all, we would like to thank Ken and Katia Holmes for translating this work. We would also like to thank Margot Newman for transcribing the tapes and Pat and Jean Johnson for helping to edit them and also Alison Morton for going over the final version. Finally, we would like to thank Sara Harding for helping correct the Tibetan.

Contents

	Foreword	vii
1.	The Precious Human Birth	1
2.	Impermanence	37
3.	Karma	53
4.	The Faults of Saṃsāra	73
	The Glossary	87
	Appendix A	94
	About the Author	96
	Index	98

Foreword

During the fifth century before our era, a tremendous explosion of philosophical thought appeared on the earth. In China Lao-tzu and Confucius were formulating a profound social and religious system which was to rule China for centuries and in Greece the beginning of "western philosophy" was being developed. In the Near East the Israelites were formulating their beliefs into a testament, and in India the Jainist and Buddhist were developing extremely complex philosophical and religious systems.

During this time, the Buddha began delivering a remarkable set of teachings. He taught that instead of relying on a god or on materialistic pursuits, one can attain true, permanent happiness by simply examining and working with one's own mind. He put forth these ideas in the very first teaching that he ever gave at the age of 35 years old in a deer park in Beneres, India. One can still visit this very place 2,500 years later and wonder what he meant by these four noble truths. He began his teaching not with an abstract theory of god or how the universe was created, but with the desire of all human beings have, namely, the desire to be happy. Next he explained that our suffering and unhappiness which we all have is do to our tendency to be attached to things. We might want to have a house and material possessions, a spouse, a feeling of respect from others, a desire to be someone important, or to have fun and enjoy ourselves. All these things are mere desires based on our concepts of what is pleasant and what is unpleasant. When we actually look around us, we find to our surprise that those who have great material wealth are no more happy than those who have next to nothing—witness primitive "stone age tribes" in the Pacific and Africa where a whole tribe might own a few dozen possessions and the people are joyous and happy. Also those who have beautiful wives and many relations are no happier that the solitary hermit practicing in his cave. Or witness those persons who are constantly partying and "having a good time" who do not feel any more satisfied in life than those who lead a more somber lifestyle. No, the Buddha said the way to achieve true and enduring happiness is not to rush headlong into external pursuits, but to lead a proper life following the eight-fold path and to examine our mind with the practice of meditation.

The Buddha continued teaching for the next fifty years and his thousands of disciples worked to preserve these teachings by not only memorizing what the Buddha had said, but also by doing the practices the Buddha suggested for reaching the state of complete and enduring happiness, the state of enlightenment. These teachings were later written down and could have easily have been lost during the Moslem invasion of India if it had not been the fact that many of these teachings were taken a few centuries earlier to Tibet and translated into Tibetan. The Tibetans were able to preserve over a hundred volumes of the direct teachings of the Buddha making a Buddhist "bible" dozens of times longer than the teachings of Lao-tzu, Moses, Jesus, Mohammed and other great religious teachers.

When Tibet became a Buddhist nation beginning in the eighth century A. D., the great practitioners and learned scholars who came from India were faced with the problem of how to convey the Buddhist teachings to a large population of traders and farmers who for the most part were illiterate. The great scholar from India Atīśa brought these four general foundations of practice to Tibet in the eleventh century. These four foundations which are identical to the "four thoughts that turn the mind towards dharma" (Tib. *lo dok namshi*) were given to the great meditator and translator Gampopa. He elaborated on these and these four thoughts have served to help thousands of students in Tibet to understand why they should begin dharma practice. Because these four thoughts are the basic reason for practicing they are said to be the four general foundations of Buddhist practice. These foundations are general to all levels and all sects of Buddhism and can be contrasted to the four special foundations (Tib. *ngöndro*) which are specific to vajrayāna Buddhism.

The first foundation or thought is the understanding of why it is important that we are born a human being and not some other animal. Being born a human also involves the obligations that come with this precious birth. The second thought is the understanding of what is permanent and worthwhile in our lives and what just comes and goes. To do anything meaningful in life, we must first understand this idea of impermanence. The third thought is the understanding of karma, which is very important because if we do not understand karma, then there is really no reason at all for leading a virtuous life, for meditating or helping others, and not just doing whatever our impulses desire. Finally, the fourth thought is that we cannot achieve any results on the Buddhist path without understanding what is wrong with our daily behavior and our present view of the world. This then is the understanding of saṃsāra.

We are pleased to have these teachings which have been passed from Gampopa right down to Thrangu Rinpoche who is a recipient of one of these long lines of transmissions. He was recognized at the age of three as the reincarnation of the previous realized Thrangu Tulku. By the age of five years, Thrangu Rinpoche was residing as head of his monastery in Tibet and was studying and memorizing vastly complicated texts. He was also practicing on the Buddhist path for his own enlightenment. Now in his fifties, Thrangu Rinpoche has devoted his entire life towards the pursuit of teaching others how to achieve enlightenment. To do this he has traveled to more than twenty different countries giving teachings and practice instructions to thousands of students in the West and the Far East.

Clark Johnson, Ph. D.
May 1, 1994

The First Reminder:

The Precious Human Life

(Tib. *mi lu rinpoche*)

The First Reminder

The Precious Human Life

(Tib. *dal ljor rinpoche*)

You are fortunate to obtain a free and well-favored (human birth)

CHAPTER 1

The Precious Human Birth

The inner expression of our being is our mind, and the outer expressions of our being are our physical actions and words. These outer expressions are much less important than the inner aspect because the mind determines the quality of our actions. So on the Buddhist path we have to work on our mind, which means turning our mind towards the *dharma*.[1] The word "dharma" has two meanings: it could mean religion in general or it could mean the teachings of the Buddha. In this context we mean the Buddhist teachings, which take the student to the highest realization. This dharma of the Buddha brings "peace," which is freedom from desire and craving and all the other negatives. The spiritual practice of the Buddha is not only going to bring peace to oneself, but it will also bring peace to other beings.

[1] Technical terms are defined in the Glossary at the end of the book.

Buddhist practice is working on the mind which means changing the mind so it turns towards the dharma. This is a process that might be easier for some and more difficult for others. Some individuals feel a natural need to leave conditioned existence (Skt. saṃsāra), behind and worldly renunciation is very easy for them. But others find that this is more difficult and they have to work on it in order to gain such a disposition. So how is it possible to change our state of mind and turn our mind away from saṃsāra? The answer is to study and meditate on the four foundations or reminders of Buddhist practice.

The first of these four foundations is the reflection on the precious human existence, which is endowed with all the freedoms and assets for achieving Buddhahood. If one has a human existence, one is very fortunate to have such an opportunity to find true happiness for all beings. Therefore, it's very rare and very precious. Without this existence, one simply becomes lost in worldly actions and this precious opportunity is wasted. That is why it is important to reflect on this first reminder of the precious human birth.

The Buddhist practice of the Kagyu lineage is the practice of the the great symbol (Skt. *mahāmudrā*), which is a very profound kind of meditation through which one can eliminate all defilements, all emotional instability, and eventually achieve the ultimate fruition of Buddhahood. But to reach this goal and to really practice mahāmudrā properly, there is a gradual stage by stage process that one has to go through.

THE PRECIOUS HUMAN BIRTH

This text[2] on meditation starts with the words, "The first meditation is to think about the difficulty of obtaining a precious human existence."

Turning Towards the Dharma

We have acquired something very precious, which is called the "precious human existence." Not only have we received this rare opportunity, but we have also entered the gates of the Buddha's teaching. Having a human existence and entering the Buddhist path is important because it is like a beginning, a possibility. However, to benefit from these conditions the mind has to have the correct attitude; so to practice the dharma properly, the mind must be directed towards the proper object, which is the dharma.

If we can turn our mind towards the dharma, then automatically all our physical actions and speech will also be turned toward the dharma. We might not immediately be able to do everything according to the dharma, but at least with the correct attitude, little by little things will improve so that in the future, all our actions will be completely in line with the dharma. If we cannot, however, turn our mind to the dharma, then things will go badly and likely worsen. They will become worse and worse because laziness will increase little by little; everything one does will

---

[2] The text which Thrangu Rinpoche used for this discussion was the last chapter of *The Torch of Certainty* by Jamgon Kongtrul. This chapter was omitted from the translation of this text by Shambhala Publications.

stray from the dharma until one's practice is no longer part of the dharma. So this is why in the beginning it is very important to direct one's mind to the dharma. This is a very basic requirement before one can truly practice.

The way to turn one's mind towards the dharma is to become aware of the qualities of the three jewels —the Buddha, the dharma and spiritual community (Skt. *sangha*). One should think about the qualities of the three jewels and think how beneficial the practice of dharma can be. However, if one does not practice dharma, one can't imagine the faults and problems that will develop from the lack of practice. By contemplating the goodness that will come out of practice of the dharma, faith in the dharma will be aroused; one will gain respect for the the Buddha who gave these teachings. One will also gain respect for those who are practicing the dharma, namely, the spiritual community. So one is trying to gain confidence, respect, and faith in the Buddha, his teachings, and those practicing the teaching. If one has strong faith in these three jewels, then one's mind will automatically turn towards the dharma. Just sitting and thinking, "I want to have faith in the dharma and I want to have confidence in the three jewels" will, of course, not get us very far. The way to develop faith in the teachings is to reflect on impermanence.

If we think about impermanence properly and deeply, we will develop faith in the three jewels. This type of reflection is necessary to have true confidence in the dharma. We can actually arouse these feelings

THE PRECIOUS HUMAN BIRTH

and let them grow to their fullness. That is why the second reminder of Buddhist practice is the reflection on impermanence. Impermanence is easy to understand because when we look around, we can see that everything is impermanent. We notice that people have to die and we can see the impermanence of our body. We can also see impermanence with our possessions. Impermanence is in everything around us, so we may think that we don't really need to think about it because it is very obvious. But we have to really contemplate it to become aware of the true implications of impermanence.

Thinking about impermanence may not be enough to prompt us to have faith in the three jewels. We may still not be aware of all the qualities of the three jewels. This is why we have to first think about the difficulty of obtaining a rare human existence. This should be done even before we think about impermanence.

Precious Human Existence

We possess what is known as the "jewel-like" (Tib. *norbu*) human body, and it is called jewel-like because it is very rare. With a human body we are extremely fortunate because we are able to practice the dharma. If we were born in a different form, we wouldn't be able to practice and gain any understanding of our condition. With a human body, however, we have an intelligent mind and a strong human body capable of sustaining effort.

This body is called a "jewel" because it is extremely valuable and rare, very beautiful and quite pure. The reason our body is called a "jewel" is twofold: we have what are known as the eight freedoms (Tib. *tel wa gye*) and what are called the ten assets or endowments (Tib. *jor wa chu*). The Tibetan word for "freedom" here literally means "ease" or "time" or the leisure to do whatever one wants. So if we need to practice dharma, or if we need to work, or do anything, we have the time to do so. The second reason for calling the body a jewel is that we have what is known as the "assets." Normally "assets" refers to any wealth or goodness. Here it means that we have all the positive circumstances that we need for our practice. We may be in a situation where we have the time to do everything we want to do, but we might find that the positive circumstance we need is not there. So here possession of assets means that we have all the positive circumstances needed to put this freedom to its full use.

When talking about the precious human existence we often refer to the six realms of saṃsāra. These six realms are the god realm (Skt. *deva*), the jealous god realm (Skt. *asura*), the human (Skt. *nara*), the animal (Skt. *tiryak*), the hungry ghost (Skt. *preta*) and the hell realms (Skt. *naraka*).[3] Human beings are only one of

[3] The Buddha suggested putting a painting of these six realms outside Buddhist temples. Realized bodhisattvas with their clairvoyance would visit these realms and return and describe them to ordinary persons. So these realms should be taken literally (rather than interpreting them as a state of ordinary mind).

THE PRECIOUS HUMAN BIRTH

these. It might be difficult at first to believe in beings that one cannot directly see, such as the hungry ghosts, beings in the hells, the jealous gods, or the gods, especially if we are new to the dharma. But there is no harm in not believing in ghosts and gods because this has to be learned about gradually.

At first it may be difficult to believe in beings from other realms, but we should remember that the reason we don't believe in these is simply because we can't see them. But if we do not see something, it doesn't automatically mean it doesn't exist. For example, if someone is sleeping, he or she may dream of many different places and people. A witness watching that person dreaming might then say, "These things don't exist," but the person dreaming is actually having a very vivid experience of these events. Because the witness is not having the same experience, he cannot deny that such experiences are possible. So because we do not see something or experience it directly, we can't deny the possibility that it is happening in the mind of other beings. Also we might have a pleasant dream of a very beautiful house located in a beautiful place containing congenial persons. But other times we have very unpleasant dreams that are frightening and painful such as being in the middle of poisonous snakes. We have these two different kinds of experiences, and what determines the quality of these experiences is entirely due to our mind. Whether we have a pleasant or unpleasant dream depends on the very fine mental imprints or subconscious traces of our mind.

A similar thing happens in our waking experiences. If we are inclined to kill and lie and steal, then these negative actions will create very strong negative traces in the mind, which will then produce very painful, frightening experiences in our next lifetime.[4] So an "evil" person will have the experiences of the hell or the animal or the hungry ghost realm because of all the negative actions the person has accumulated in the previous lifetime.

In contrast, if someone in a given lifetime has practiced generosity and right conduct, then that person will have experience as a human being, a jealous god, or a god in another lifetime, which is pleasant and agreeable. So the process of karma is very much like a dream; the traces left by one's previous actions affect whether one will have pleasant or unpleasant dreams, and everything we experience in waking is the product of our previous actions. This is why the Buddha gave the teaching on the six realms of saṃsāra. He gave these teachings not to make people afraid, but to tell them the way the world really works.

We are human beings, which means we are in a very fortunate situation because we do not have to go through the experiences of less favorable realms. We are, in fact, in the best possible realm. For instance, imagine how much suffering the life of an animal entails. In the short-term an animal has to endure a

[4] Buddhists believe in reincarnation with one's karma passing on from one lifetime to the next.

lot of pain and difficulty that it cannot avoid. In the long-term an animal is unable to set goals or work towards a better life or any form of liberation. An animal is also unable to think intelligently so that it cannot alleviate its condition. In these terms humans are much more fortunate because they are mentally and physically equipped to improve their state, evolve, and progress. And, of course, if we compare ourselves to beings in the hell realm or hungry ghost realm, we realize just how fortunate we are.

The Eight Freedoms

Human beings have the eight freedoms which means they are free from the eight unfavorable conditions.

The first unfavorable condition is to be born in the hell realms. If one is in the hell realm, one can suffer from either extreme heat or tremendous cold. Whichever way one suffers, one finds that one is continually imprisoned in excruciating suffering and there is nothing to relieve it. Even if someone in hell had the inclination to practice the dharma, he or she would never have a chance to do so because there is constant suffering. In comparison, we as human beings are extremely fortunate because we do not have this intense suffering and we have the possibility of doing whatever we want in terms of dharma practice.

One might think that the hell realm is really an extreme example and that there might be some other realm that is better. But let us examine what happens to the hungry ghosts. It is certainly not better because people born into this realm go through continual intense starvation and thirst, so the only thing they can think of is trying to find food and drink. Hungry ghosts are constantly preoccupied with finding food and drink, and they cannot think of anything else, not even the dharma. They are so deprived that they can never do anything useful with their body or their speech. In contrast, we are fortunate because we do not have such suffering and hardships and are able to do what we want.

Is it any better in the animal realm? No, it isn't, because animals are afflicted by very strong stupidity. They can't think intelligently so that they can never direct their minds towards anything constructive. They can't think, "I want to practice" or really understand someone telling them to practice. Even if they are told, "I will give you one thousand ounces of gold if you practice the dharma or repeat "OṀ MAṆI PADME HŪṀ."[5] they are totally unable to repeat or understand it. Even if one threatens the animal with "If you don't say 'OṀ MAṆI PADME HŪṀ,' I'm going to kill you," the poor thing can't do anything because it doesn't understand what it was told. In contrast, we are so fortunate because we can think, we can understand, and we have the possibility of creating the cause for our future happiness by practicing virtue and eliminating unvirtuous actions.

[5] This is the mantra of Avalokiteśvara (Tib. *Chenrezig*) who represents compassion.

Fourth, we are fortunate because we were not born in the three lower states. Being born as a human being doesn't automatically imply that we will be able to practice the dharma. The dharma has to be present in the country where we are living. And the dharma has to be very prevalent, because if it is confined to a very small area of a country, it is likely we won't ever hear about it and will never get to know about it. Even if we knew about the dharma in this country, we probably wouldn't be able to practice. Persons in such situations are referred to as "barbarians" in the Buddhist teachings. These are people who are in a culture where there is no chance of encountering the dharma and practicing it properly. In contrast, we are lucky because we are in a situation where we are exposed to the dharma and can practice it.

Fifth, the gods in the god realm have a very pleasant life where they enjoy all kinds of sensual things, much more than human beings. But these beings reached the god realm because they were involved in a concentration which was oriented only to worldly things, and they are totally engrossed with pleasurable things. Because they are so caught up with materialism, they do not have the wish to look for anything else, so it doesn't occur to them that they could find liberation and become buddhas. In comparison, we are very lucky because we haven't been born as gods and we have the opportunity to practice.

Sixth, another reason why we are fortunate to be human beings is that we could have been born in a place where there was no dharma, with the word "dharma" meaning having no good religion. There are all kinds of religions; some good, some bad. There is, for instance, the mistaken religious belief that it is good to kill animals, that is to sacrifice them. There are all kinds of mistaken beliefs and we are very lucky because we have a religion without any of these incorrect beliefs. The religion we have is a pure one. It's the teachings of the Buddha; a teaching meant to bring peace, a teaching which has been around for 2,500 years with a practice that leads to complete realization. We are able to see for ourselves how this teaching has brought so many beings to Buddhahood and how these teachings can help so many other beings to reach Buddhahood on the way. So we are very fortunate because we are not involved in a misguided religion and we can follow the religion of the Buddha, which is a pure teaching.

The seventh unfavorable circumstance is to find oneself in a world where no Buddha has manifested. If this is the case, then one doesn't know about the Buddha, one doesn't know about the dharma, because there has been no one to teach it. One doesn't know about the sangha because there's no one to practice the teachings. So there is a complete ignorance of the three jewels. In contrast, we find ourselves in circumstances where the Buddha has come to our world and given teachings. We can receive these teachings, practice them, and have the chance to realize them.

The eighth unfavorable circumstance is being born mentally deficient. Some persons are born mentally deficient and cannot understand what other people are trying to tell them. Of course, if one is mentally deficient there is little hope of understanding the dharma and even less of practicing it. So we are fortunate because we were born with normal intellectual ability and intact faculties.

The eight favorable circumstances are avoiding the eight unfavorable circumstances and as a result possessing the eight freedoms. These eight freedoms are a very great gift because if one possesses these eight, then one is able to reach Buddhahood. All the buddhas and *bodhisattvas* of the past possessed these eight freedoms, and these are what made it possible for them to reach realization. Likewise, if we possess these eight freedoms, there is nothing more that we need, and we find ourselves in the same situation as all those buddhas and bodhisattvas when they first set out on the Buddhist path. What we need to do is to become aware of these eight freedoms and then to apply as much effort as is required to reach the realization of a Buddha.

The Eight Obstacles to Practice

We have been fortunate enough to be free of the eight unfavorable conditions. Being free from these, we have this precious human existence with all the freedoms and all the assets. We have even more than this because we have begun to study the teachings of the Buddha and aspire to practice the dharma. When we realize all these incredible possibilities, we should be extremely happy. We should realize just how fortunate we are to possess this very rare opportunity of having all these possibilities gathered together. Once we truly realize this, then we should determine not to let it go to waste but to use it properly so we will have the greatest benefit, not only for ourselves, but for all sentient beings.

Possessing these favorable circumstances does not automatically mean that we will always have them in the future. If we do not use this opportunity now, later we may not find such an opportunity. This thought should stop the temptation of laziness. So it is important to know this, and knowing it, to work on it. If we can meditate on this point, we will become aware of how fortunate we are that we are able to work on obtaining true happiness. This should give us encouragement to be diligent and develop a strong determination to really use this possibility.

When we practice the dharma, we encounter some obstacles, some difficulties. One obstacle is the temptation to put oneself down, to think that we are not really capable of properly doing anything. For instance, we may think "Well, other people can receive teachings and understand them, but I can't. Somehow, I will never make it. They can meditate and get good results with their meditation, but I'm not able to do this. Other people can eliminate their negativities, but I'm not able to do this. Some beings are even able to reach Buddhahood and become great bodhisattvas, but this is totally beyond my reach." If we start thinking like this, it will paralyze us completely, and we will be unable to practice. What we must think in such a case is that there is absolutely no reason for us to be depressed or to put ourselves down because we possess the most precious thing— the precious human existence which is endowed with all the possibilities and qualities needed for real, full liberation. We must think that now we have this potential, we can use it, and there's no reason why we can't gain miraculous powers and the complete understanding of phenomena. All we need to do is to work on it with much diligence. When we think about all these assets, it will encourage us not to feel discouraged and depressed.

The Eight Unfavorable Circumstances

The first unfavorable circumstance occurs when the five poisons (Skt. *kleśas*) are very strong. This occurs when one feels very strong bursts of anger, desire, stupidity, jealously, or pride. Although one has this precious human existence and wishes to practice dharma, sometimes these very violent, negative feelings arise and one feels totally overpowered by them. These very strong feelings make one want to just give up practice of the dharma. When this happens, one must be extremely careful to see what is happening and then to apply a remedy with great diligence and perseverance.[6]

[6]The antidotes to these difficulties are described in Thrangu Rinpoche's *The Practice of Tranquillity and Insight*. Boston, Mass.: Shambhala Publications.

The second unfavorable circumstance is the influence of bad friends. Even though one knows that the dharma is beneficial and wishes to practice, one may fall under the influence of a bad friend who makes one stop practicing. This may be a friend who has the influence to make one drop one's practice and to act harmfully, even though one doesn't really want to. This is a very strong danger to one's practice. What one has to do is to examine oneself to see whether one is likely to fall under such an influence and if there is presently something in one's life that might cause this. If one feels that there is no such danger, then one should rejoice and decide to strive even more strongly in one's practice. But if one sees that there is perhaps a danger, then one should start thinking of a way in which one can eliminate the negative influence.

The third unfavorable circumstance is not clearly knowing what is a danger and what is a help to one's practice. Not knowing what might threaten and what might benefit one's practice will result in not knowing how to direct one's efforts so one might end up trying to get rid of things that are good and cultivating things that are bad. If one does that, of course, one's practice will be misguided and this will become an obstacle to proper practice. So one must examine oneself, and if one finds such a danger, then one should employ the remedy of studying the dharma more thoroughly and learning very precisely what one has to practice and what one has to avoid, and then act accordingly. If one does this, one will find that it is much easier to practice because one knows exactly what to do.

The fourth unfavorable circumstance that may arise is falling under the influence of laziness. One may have the wish to practice but sometimes one may become really lazy and this inertia will stop one's practice. Even if one manages to practice, it will be very little and one will always feel, "Oh, I can do that tomorrow" or "I can do that later" so one's practice makes little progress and in the end one might stop practicing altogether. So if one finds that this obstacle is stopping one's practice, one has to be determined that one won't fall under the influence of laziness, and push constantly to generate a little more effort, and be a little more diligent in practicing.

The fifth unfavorable circumstance that may arise is encountering unfavorable results from previous karma, that is, deeds from a previous lifetime that come to fruition in this lifetime. One may suddenly experience very great problems in one's practice such as a sudden illness. When this happens, one should think that it is the result of some bad deeds in some previous lifetime and try to remedy these bad results. The first thing to do is to try to purify the bad actions one has committed by means of confession and purification. If one does this it will help overcome these difficulties a little. If these problems are so large that they stop one from practicing completely, one must continue hoping and praying that they will come to an end quickly; then as soon as the difficulty preventing one from practicing has gone, one immediately resumes one's practice with as much diligence as possible.

The sixth unfavorable circumstance is that one is not one's own master and is dependent on someone else. Even though one may have the wish to practice the dharma, whoever is controlling one may stop one from practicing or even entering the dharma. If the situation continues, one should realize that one's very precious human existence endowed with all the qualities could be wasted. The remedy is to eliminate this controlling interference and to become one's own master and begin to practice.

The seventh obstacle is impure motivation. One might want to or actually be practicing the dharma, but behind one's practice there is impure motivation. With such impure motivation the result of one's practice will not be very great. Examples of impure motivations are thinking, "If I don't practice the dharma, I am going to be poor in the next life and I don't want to be poor, so I'm going to practice" or thinking "I do not want to become sick and suffer in this life so I want to practice dharma." Of course, there will be some benefit from this limited motivation, but real benefit comes from desiring to lead other beings to ultimate happiness. If one finds that one has an impure motivation, one must try to eliminate it or change it into a pure motivation aimed at reaching Buddhahood in order to help all beings.

The last unfavorable circumstance is also caused by an impure motivation. This is practicing with a very immediate goal in mind. For example, doing good things to become famous or to profit directly from what one is doing, like expecting money or reward from the activity. For instance, some people give very generously but expect great fame or reward in return. So whenever one does something good or practices the dharma with the expectation of an immediate benefit, it is an impure motivation. This kind of practice is very deceptive because from the outside it looks authentic and people will think it's genuine dharma practice because this person is performing good things. But it is only make-believe dharma. So when one finds that there might be some of this in one's attitude, one should really try to give it up at all costs because otherwise one will be wasting the precious jewel of human existence.

These eight unfavorable circumstances to our practice are just incidental unfavorable conditions and are not solid; they just happen from time to time. What we have to do is to remain vigilant and examine ourselves from time to time to see whether any of these difficulties have appeared. If they have, we have to try to eliminate them so they will not interrupt our practice. We should use these eight points for meditation. We should examine ourselves to find whether any of these eight temporary difficulties are present. The main problem to our practice is laziness. If we don't examine ourselves to find if there is anything wrong, we will very quickly fall under the power of laziness and won't do anything to remedy our difficulties. So it is very important to go through each one of these eight difficulties and look at each one and think, "Do I have this difficulty? Is it present in me?" When we go through each of them, we may find that one is present here, another one there. Then systematically we should apply the remedy that is necessary to eliminate this temporary difficulty. And if we can manage to eliminate it, we will be able to practice. If we don't do anything about it, then we will just become lazy and there won't be any true practice.

The Eight Mental Obstacles

In addition, to the eight unfavorable circumstances and the eight obstacles to practice, there is a third set of conditions dependent entirely on one's way of thinking that are not the result of one's birth or nature. These eight unfavorable conditions are due to one's way of thinking. Sometimes one has thoughts that lead one away from the correct way of practicing. Mistaken ways of thinking will create obstacles to one's practice, so it is important to examine oneself to see if one has any of these mistakes or faults. If one can recognize them, then one will be able to eliminate them and be free from the obstacles they pose.

The first mental obstacle is becoming very attached to possessions, or esteem and money, or relatives and friends. If one is very strongly involved with one's possessions, one will be constantly in fear of losing them or always be hoping to get more possessions. Being involved with possessions doesn't give the mind any space or time for anything else, so this involvement with wealth becomes an obstacle to the practice of dharma. One becomes a slave thinking about one's possessions so that one doesn't have any time or opportunity to practice. If one is involved with one's family or a close friend, one will be so involved that one won't be able to leave them and take time to practice and little by little one will end up dropping one's practice. However, one's possessions or family or friends are not bad in themselves. There is a need to have some money, some possessions simply to live, and it is good to love people and be kind to them. But a problem arises when one becomes too attached to them. Even though one is free to practice because of the two different aspects of freedom, one is not able to do so because one is so attached to the things or people one likes that one drops practice. It therefore becomes an obstacle, so it has to be abandoned.

The second obstacle is behaving in an extremely negative way. Someone with very strong anger and negativity will find it extremely difficult to have a decent relationship with his or her lama. They will be constantly fighting with dharma friends and the situation will become so difficult that they will be totally unable to practice because the negativity is so strong. If this happens, of course, the most important thing is to become aware of it. Once one is aware of it, one has to work on eliminating it, which one has to do by oneself. Of course, learning how to meditate will help, but trying to eliminate all of this extreme negativity is something one has to start doing oneself. Not eliminating this obstacle will result in loss of the freedom to practice. Therefore, it is important to examine oneself to see if one has this problem, and if one does, to correct it.

The third mental obstacle is being unafraid of the suffering saṃsāra and not feeling any wish to abandon suffering. Persons like this are still not frightened or dissatisfied with their existence even if they see or hear of all the sufferings of the lower states. They still don't really care because they believe everything is suffering anyway. They don't feel that their behavior makes any difference and consequently they have no wish to be liberated and, of course, won't try to practice the dharma. Without practicing the dharma, there is no way to gain liberation. So if one thinks such a thought, one should eliminate it and change it into a wish to practice based on the fear of all the suffering of saṃsāra. Eliminating this hindrance, then, frees one to practice and achieve liberation.

The fourth mental obstacle is not having enough faith. One may hear about all the qualities of the dharma and how, if practiced, it can bring liberation, and still not feel any faith or real conviction that one can achieve Buddhahood. It is as though one's mind is blocking the door to liberation. If this happens, one has to eliminate that thought and then one will obtain the fourth freedom from mental obstacles.

The fifth mental obstacle is enjoying aggressive actions. Some people who are not spiritually mature find themselves going on the wrong path. They don't have any particular reason for acting badly, but they just enjoy killing, lying, stealing, etc. The most serious ones are the five actions of immediate result[7] which bring an immediate rebirth in the lower realms. Everything a person does with this tendency in his actions, his speech and his thinking will be negative. Such a person cannot practice the dharma or find any peace. However, under some favorable circumstances, the person will be able to see that this is wrong and seeing this, it will be possible to change this wrong attitude and eliminate this obstacle to spiritual practice. If one can do this, then one gains the fifth freedom from mental obstacles.

The sixth mental obstacle is a natural dislike of the dharma. Even though others might point out that dharma is very beneficial, this person won't feel that it is worth it. The person doesn't have any particular reason, it's just that they don't see that it is good. It is like giving grass to a dog. The dog doesn't think, "Oh, this is grass and I don't like grass," it just doesn't eat it. In the same way, these people might have the dharma in front of them, and an opportunity to hear teachings and to practice, but they do not see how it could help them and be useful. They don't have enough spiritual maturity to understand the opportunity. But this lack of maturity is only a thought and under favorable circumstances one can realize that it is only a thought that is blocking practice, and one can eliminate this unfavorable mental

---

[7] These are killing one's father, killing one's mother, killing an arhat, intentionally wounding a bodhisattva until he or she bleeds, and causing disharmony in the Buddhist sangha.

circumstance and gain the sixth freedom from mental obstacles.

The seventh mental obstacle is having taken vows and commitments and broken them without doing anything to repair them. For instance someone has taken the commitment to bring all beings to enlightenment (the bodhisattva vow) or taken some of the *prātimokṣa* vows[8] and breaks these vows and doesn't bother to do anything about it. Under these circumstances the wish to practice properly will be impaired. Of course, breaking vows happens to almost everyone, but it is important to want to remedy them. So if that obstacle arises, one has to become aware of it and do everything that is necessary to purify and repair the breaking of the vows and commitments.

The eighth mental obstacle is that someone out of a dislike for the teacher or dharma friends breaks his or her commitments and forsakes the practice completely. This strong dislike for the teacher or for the people who are studying under the teacher causes the person to abandon the practice completely. When this happens there is no way for the person to practice any more, and this becomes an obstacle in which the person loses the opportunity to practice and to gain liberation. But if this person becomes aware of the

---

[8]Lay persons can take up to seven vows such as to not to kill, to steal, the lie, engage in sexual misconduct, take intoxicants while fully ordained monks and nuns take over a hundred vows.

THE PRECIOUS HUMAN BIRTH 25

problem and does what is necessary in order to repair these broken commitments, then he or she can again practice and receive all the benefits of practice and gain the eighth freedom.

Summary

We have just seen that there are two sets of immediate obstacles to practice. The first set was the eight temporary unfavorable circumstances. The second set was the eight obstacles caused by our mind. If individuals have not begun in the dharma, there is no concern for the obstacles. For those who have already started, the obstacles will interrupt or cause them to leave the dharma. Therefore, it is very important not to allow these difficulties to arise or if they have arisen, to eliminate them.

Since we are ordinary beings, it is only very natural that we will meet with obstacles from time to time. But the important thing is to try to become aware of these obstacles, because if we aren't aware of the obstacles, they will have produced a negative effect and stopped our practice before we can do anything. So always be very careful and try to see if there are any of these difficulties. If we find that we have made a terrible mistake, we mustn't feel there's nothing we can do or that now our practice is completely spoiled. We must say we are aware of the mistake, can correct it, and start anew to work on spiritual practice again.

This teaching on the precious human existence teaches that there are eight freedoms. In more detail these eight basic freedoms are added to eight freedoms from temporary difficulties and eight freedoms from mental obstacles. So to be in a really good position to practice the dharma, we have to be free from the twenty-four unfavorable conditions. If we can be free from any of these problems, then our practice will be very fruitful, and we will be able to achieve liberation.

The Five External Assets

There are ten assets—five of which come from oneself and five which come from others. We should go through each of these different points and try to examine ourself for these obstacles in our life and determine whether we really possess all the freedoms and assets. If we possess them all, then we should feel very lucky because we have a complete opportunity to practice. Having entered the dharma, we can develop the habit of virtue so things will get better and better and we will improve more and more, not just in this life, but from one lifetime to the next.

On the other hand, if someone cultivates bad habits, then the negativity will also accrue, becoming worse and worse and bringing about more and more suffering for oneself. This is why it is so important to keep on checking to see if one is in full possession of these freedoms and assets. One of the elements might be missing due to a mental cause, such as a wrong way of thinking, but it could also be due to something outside of oneself. In either case one should

THE PRECIOUS HUMAN BIRTH

acknowledge the missing asset and try to change it so one is again in full possession of all the freedoms and assets to insure that one is leaving suffering behind.

The second kind of assets are those that come from someone or some circumstance outside of ourselves. The first of these is that a Buddha must have come into the world where one is living. At the present time, we live in a world where the Buddha Śākyamuni came and gave teachings, which means that we are spiritually mature enough to be able to come in contact with those teachings and practice them. There hasn't always been a Buddha present; for instance, the universe at the beginning of its formation did not have a Buddha because there weren't enough beings ready to practice and mature enough to understand the teachings of the Buddha. So a Buddha comes when there are beings to be taught. Once the Buddha has come, then after a time, like a few thousand years after his coming, the presence of the teachings will begin to wane and the teaching will disappear altogether. But we are extremely fortunate to live at a time and in a world where the teachings of the Buddha are present.

We are living in a good eon (Skt. *kalpa*) in which a thousand buddhas are predicted to come, with some having already come.[9] So the Buddha that we study is the Buddha Śākyamuni who was born in 563 B. C. in India and who manifested enlightenment in India.

[9] In this eon there was the previous Kāshyapa Buddha, the present Shākyamuni Buddha and the future Maitreya Buddha. Also Padmasambhava is considered a Buddha in Tibet.

This Buddha gave teachings that correspond to the various levels of maturity of beings. We now have these teachings and can practice them, so we have the first asset of depending on others.

The second asset is that the Buddha who has come into our world has given teachings. The Buddha or bodhisattva or *śrāvaka* may be born into a world and may develop direct realization of the nature of all phenomena, but may not teach this to others. Or they may give only short teachings without many details not allowing beings to receive the full benefit of the teachings because there is no way to practice. If a Buddha teaches only little, there is the danger that his teachings will decline and disappear very quickly.

When Buddha Śākyamuni first manifested enlightenment, he remained for quite a long time without teaching. He realized the uncreated quality of the nature of all phenomena, but he wondered whether anyone would be able to understand it. At first he felt, "I am not going to teach. I will just remain in meditation and not give any teachings" and remained silent for seven weeks. But quite a few gods and other nonhuman beings could see this, and they came to supplicate the Buddha and request him to give teachings. In the end the Buddha began to teach. This is why we have the second asset of the teachings of the Buddha.

We live at a time when we have all the teachings of the Buddha. The Buddha turned the wheel of dharma (Skt. *dharmacakra*), giving the teachings of the *hīnayāna*, of the *mahāyāna*, and of the *vajrayāna* so that

THE PRECIOUS HUMAN BIRTH

all of us have the possibility of practicing whatever aspect of the dharma is most suited to us. But sometimes even very great teachers give a teaching to others, but find the people are not ready for this teaching, so they will not teach.

There was a great Indian teacher who was called Richijana. This teacher was very learned and also quite realized. Through his clairvoyance he saw that his mother had been reborn as a frog enclosed inside a stone in Tibet. Moved by very great compassion, he thought that he should go there and try to help his mother. He set out on the road to Tibet accompanied by an interpreter because he didn't know Tibetan. But on the way his interpreter died, so when he reached Tibet, he couldn't speak a word of Tibetan. He ended up working as a goatherd, and so all these great teachings were just wasted because nobody had any idea that he was a great teacher. Later, another very great teacher came from India, and when he recognized this great teacher he said, "What a shame such a great teacher as you is wasted like this. You could be giving all these great teachings. Truly the people of Tibet are not very spiritually mature or positively endowed because they are not able to benefit from your teachings." As the Indian teacher was saying this, he had tears in his eyes and bowed down in respect to this other teacher because he realized just how much was wasted because there was no situation that made teaching possible.

The Buddha has come into our world and given teachings. This third asset is that these teachings shouldn't decline and disappear. If this happens, it is the same as if the Buddha hadn't come in the first place, because without the teachings, one doesn't know how to practice. The country of India was called "the noble land" or the "very excellent land" because it was the country where the Buddha's teachings were spreading and it was a very spiritual country. When the hīnayāna teachings spread, many, many beings achieved arhatship as a result of practice. Then when there was the great wave of mahāyāna, many, many beings realized the state of a bodhisattva. When the vajrayāna teachings spread, many beings achieved the state of mahāsiddha. But little by little all these great teachings waned and became less and less important until in the end they disappeared completely and the people in India did not have the karma to practice and were deprived from the opportunity of practicing. As a result the dharma disappeared from India.

However, the Buddhist teachings were introduced into Tibet by Khenpo Bodhisattva, Padmasambhava, and king Thrisong Detsen in the ninth century A. D. Under the influence of these three, the dharma came to Tibet and flourished under four main schools of Buddhism in Tibet. And within each of these schools were very great mahāsiddhas, very learned teachers, and extremely gifted meditators. But little by little the teachings disappeared so that in the end, the people were deprived from this opportunity of practicing. Now in Tibet the dharma isn't there and there's no longer the opportunity to practice. But here in the

THE PRECIOUS HUMAN BIRTH

West and Far East the teachings are present and we have this opportunity to practice.

The expansion of the dharma in an area is due to two factors. It is the result of the activity of the compassion of the buddhas and bodhisattvas. It is also due to the good karma of the people who receive the teachings. When these two factors are present, the dharma spreads in that area. For instance, many dharma centers in the West have been established and the teachings of the Buddha are spreading. They now have all the positive conditions—teachers who give teachings so that they can receive these teachings and can work in harmony with the dharma. They can meditate and do activities such as saying Avalokiteśvara's (Tib. *Chenrezig*) mantra (OM MANI PADME HŪM) or Padmasambhava's (Tib. *Guru Rinpoche*) mantra ("OM AH HŪM VAJRA GURU PADMA SIDDHI HŪM").

So one has this opportunity to practice the dharma in all its aspects because one has a special readiness for it. These teachings of the dharma are the fruition of one's previous good karma, but also the fruition of one's present aspiration to practice and follow the Buddha. Because of all of this, one is extremely fortunate and should use this good fortune to practice properly.

The fourth asset is that the dharma is practiced. First a Buddha has to enter the world, second he has to give teachings, and then third the teachings must be present. The fourth condition is that the teachings must be practiced, because even if one has the best teaching, if no one practices, nothing will result. For example, no matter how bright and free from clouds the sun is, the sunlight will never reach a person living deep inside a cave. Even though the sun is everywhere, a person has to come out of the cave to feel it. So the teachings can be present everywhere through the activity of the Buddha, but they have to be practiced to be useful.

We are very fortunate because we have entered the path of the dharma and started practicing. Western countries are very rich, and it is possible to accumulate a great deal of wealth, so it is quite tempting to get into the "rat race" to try to acquire more wealth and to become distracted by material pursuits. However, we are fortunate because we haven't gotten completely carried away and have managed to enter the dharma path and started to practice. Some may tell us, "This dharma practice of yours is not very useful; you won't get very much out of it." But you mustn't listen to what other people tell you and look for yourself to realize just how lucky you are that you are actually able to start practicing dharma, because you'll see the benefits for yourself.

The fifth asset is being helped by the kindness of other people. More precisely, without the kindness of our teachers, it would be very difficult to practice. We need someone who will encourage us to practice, help us to enter the path, and follow us through our progress on the path. So there are quite a few teachers who have come and are giving teachings and can help us in our practice. This constitutes the fifth asset, people who out of kindness are ready to help us with our practice.

Summary

The first topic of meditation is precious human existence endowed with all freedoms and assets. This is like a jewel and is very precious because it is very difficult to find. If we don't have a human existence, then it is impossible to practice the dharma, because we must know what is virtuous and what is unvirtuous to practice the dharma. We see that all other forms of life, especially animals, cannot do this. An animal is incapable of acting in the right way either with its body or speech and can't even meditate. On the contrary, animals have a natural tendency to do harmful actions as the result of previous karma. They kill and steal because they don't have anyone to teach them.

Our precious human existence is the result of our previous good actions. To gather all the good conditions making a human birth possible is quite difficult. It requires a great amount of good karma and receiving the blessing of the Buddha. So a human birth is indeed a very rare thing when it occurs and is not guaranteed for future lifetimes. If we use this human life to practice properly, we will have the opportunity from one life to the next to reduce suffering more and more, not just for ourselves, but also for all other beings. But if we don't use our human birth to practice the dharma, then most likely things will not be very good afterwards.

The Second Reminder:

Impermanence

(Tib. *chiwa mitakpa*)

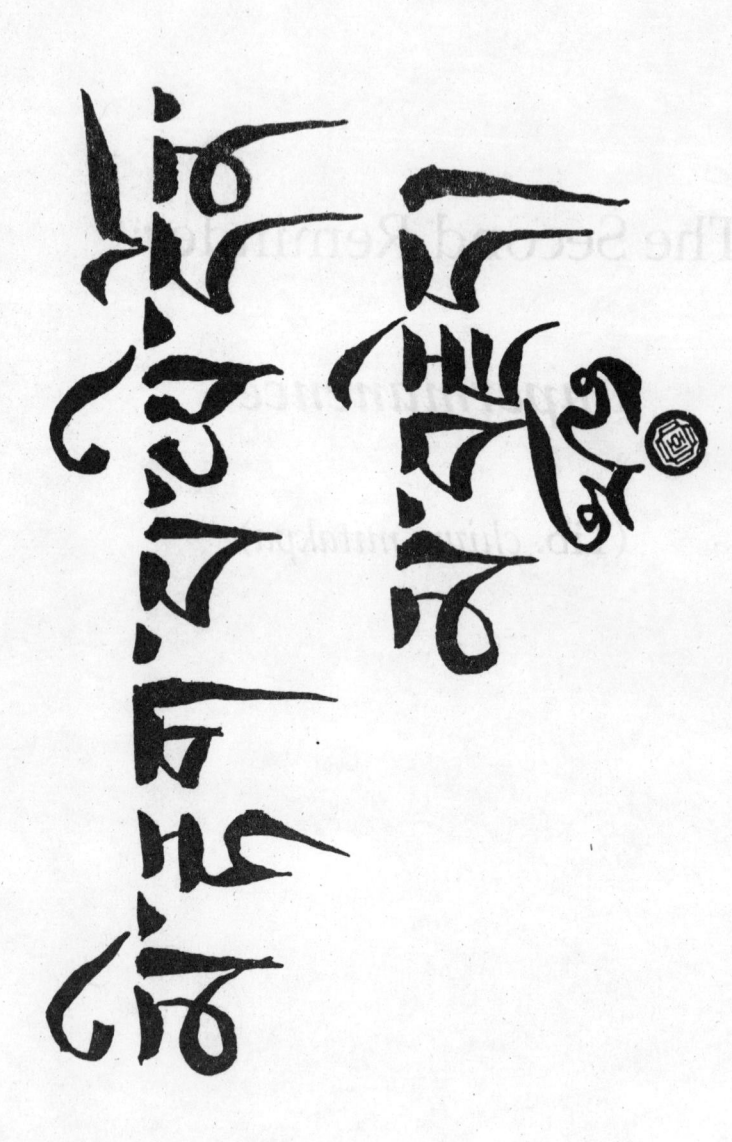

Don't forget the meaning of impermanence

CHAPTER 2

Impermanence

Once one understands how rare and precious human existence is, one must also understand that one must use it to practice the dharma. Some people may feel that they can take their time, practicing little by little without much rush. This is a real mistake because nothing is permanent. Everything passes, everything changes, so we must use this opportunity quickly while we can. This is why the second reminder of meditation is impermanence.

The study of impermanence will really help to turn one's mind to the dharma quickly. Once one knows just how much everything changes, one becomes aware that one can't afford to waste time. Some people might think that impermanence is just a clever device used by the Buddha to scare people into practicing right away. But this isn't so. Impermanence is an intrinsic feature of life; our life is changeable and destructible. So the idea of impermanence wasn't made up.

Believing that everything will last forever is a mistake. To correct this mistake, one has to realize that everything is impermanent. One may think that meditation on impermanence is unpleasant because it means that everything will disintegrate and end. This is true, but extremely important. Becoming aware of the impermanence of everything will not make one feel wonderful and happy.

Suppose we go to a place with a tiger, but we don't know of the presence of the tiger. So we are enjoying the place and thinking that it is so very nice there. Then the tiger appears and by then it is too late. So we have to go through the terrific fear of suddenly seeing a tiger jumping out at us and then being eaten up by it. However, if we know that there is a tiger there, then we can avoid going there. Of course, knowing about the tiger means that at the beginning we will have that fear of the tiger. So we will have a fairly unpleasant feeling of fear thinking there's a tiger there and how to avoid it. But because we are aware of the presence of the tiger, we will be able to avoid the real danger.

Normally people just take life as it comes and goes and are involved with their daily activities. There are always many things to do and they don't think that everything changes and goes. So without thinking, this life may feel very pleasant and undisturbed by thoughts of things disintegrating, changing, or being lost. But whether one is aware of impermanence or not, it doesn't make any difference because not knowing about impermanence is not going to stop it. When impermanence occurs, it will be there and if it takes us by surprise, it will be extremely painful. However, if we know about impermanence, we will be prepared for it and with practice, we will be able to overcome whatever difficulties come from impermanence. We should use the instructions given by the Buddha and all the lamas that came before us to see how everything around us changes and is impermanent. This is true of our life; nothing remains the same forever. At first this thought might generate a lot of unhappiness because it is not very pleasant to think about. But if we are prepared, when impermanence comes and strikes us, it won't be very painful. Through our practice we work towards the ultimate form of happiness, the one that never changes.

Meditation on impermanence is useful at all stages of one's practice. It's useful when one just enters the practice of the dharma because it turns one's mind to the dharma very quickly. But it is also useful when one is already practicing when comes under the influence of laziness by renewing one's wish to practice. So we think about impermanence from time to time to renew our enthusiasm in our practice. Thinking about impermanence is useful for reaching our goal very quickly. It is like a friend that helps us reach the goal quickly.

Meditation on Impermanence

How does one meditate on impermanence? In the instructions that are given in the preliminary practices (Tib. *ngöndro*[10]) of mahāmudrā it says, "The world and all its inhabitants is impermanent. In particular, the life of beings is like a bubble in water. It is uncertain when I will die and become a corpse. As it is only the dharma that can help me at that time, I must practice now with diligence." This is summarized in the ngöndro text by five main points which are the key to the five ways of meditating on impermanence.

First meditation on impermanence is on the changing nature of everything. By nature everything changes, and this applies to the world and to the beings who inhabit it. The world around us is always changing. In the summer, nature has certain colors, certain appearances, and these change gradually. It becomes different in autumn and autumn will not remain forever. The features of autumn will be replaced by winter and winter has special characteristics, and these also will gradually change and be replaced by spring. So we can see that everything

---

[10]In Tibet one usually begins Buddhist practice with ngöndro. This consists of doing about 100,000 prostrations, then 100,000 vajrasattva mantras, 100,000 maṇḍala offerings, and 100,000 guru yoga supplications. This is common to all sects in Tibet but there are variations of these.

IMPERMANENCE

around us changes gradually and continuously. There isn't one thing that is not subject to change.

Now if we examine persons, they also are subject to change. Take, for example, our body. When we were children, our body had a certain size, a certain appearance, and we thought in a certain way. Then when we grew a bit older and became young adults and later middle aged people, our size and our appearance changed, and our thinking changed. In old age one is different again. Finally, we will die and disintegrate. We can see this change very clearly in the people we know, and we know some who have grown very old and some who have already died. We can see that there is a constant process of change and this impermanence is really part of the nature of all things around us. Obviously we aren't making this up; it is an inherent part of nature. Because all things change, we cannot rely on them. The only thing that can be of use is something that doesn't change, and that is the dharma. Only our practice of dharma can help us.

The second meditation on impermanence is to reflect on the death of others and how we also will die. We can see other persons born at the same time as us who are already dead, and some of them will die soon, and we will also die. We might think that death applies to others, but there is nothing that says everyone else will die except us. If we were somehow the exception and were not going to die, we would not have to do any practice. We wouldn't need to worry and could be involved in anything we wanted.

But there is no exception for us and we are like everyone else. From the beginning of time, there hasn't been a single person who hasn't undergone death. We might say, "Well, I haven't met someone who won't die, but that doesn't necessarily imply there isn't such a person." But even if we haven't met such a person, if he or she existed, we surely would have heard about such an exceptional person. There is no need for one to entertain any doubt about it: Death applies to everyone. All those who have been born in the past have died; all those in the future will also die. Why do all these people die? It is because of impermanence.

The Buddha said that it is not important to be attached to food, money, clothes, or possessions. It isn't important because these things that should give us pleasure are not permanent. Whatever we own will not be of any use when we die. Whether we are wealthy or famous, when we die, it makes no difference at all. The only thing that helps us when we die is whatever virtue we have been able to accumulate during our life. If we have been able to generate a lot of very good positive spiritual energy, it will help us when we die. But all our worldly possessions or fame won't make a difference. This is why it is said that practicing the dharma is of much greater importance than any other endeavor we can engage in during our life on this planet.

We may believe that we have a lot of time ahead of us before death and that later on we can start practicing. But we really cannot have such confidence.

There's absolutely no reason why we should feel this because we cannot tell when we are going to die. It could be very soon or it could happen very quickly and it could happen after a few years. But at any rate, even if we live a long time, it will never be for a very, very long time in terms of thousands of years.

So time is a very important factor in our life and is very precious. If we waste time, even a short time, then it is time during which we could have been practicing and getting closer to our goal. With some effort we can use that time to achieve our goal. Getting lost in worldly pursuits is very much like children who are playing and forget everything else but their games. If we do this, we won't be able to achieve very much in worldly terms or be able to do much good for ourselves or others. So it's important not to waste our time and to try to use it for a more fruitful endeavor, which is dharma practice.

Many Causes of Death

The third main instruction for meditation on impermanence is to realize that there are many different causes of death. Our life is not very stable because our birth was brought about by many different conditions. Because we are made up of so many different elements and created through many different conditions, our life is a composite and not very stable. Any composite is likely to decompose again. We can't make this unstable combination of elements more stable. We can, however, learn how not to dwell in fear and use this awareness of the coming of death to practice and work towards real happiness, so when death strikes there will be happiness without pain. There are many causes of death. When we talk about death, it's not like parents who tell their little child not to go into a particular house because there is a tiger in there to keep the child out of there when, in fact, there is no tiger. Instead we should think that death is inevitable and through this awareness, we will realize that what is really meaningful in our life is our practice of dharma, and that strong involvement with our ordinary life is quite useless and pointless because it doesn't help us with death.

First of all, there are things such as food, money, possessions, friends, and our families which are meant to help us live better. But we have to realize that sometimes these things can also cause death. Normally, we need food to survive and grow. But food can sometimes turn into poison and we can die from it. The same is true of money and possessions; they might make life better, but sometimes they could be the cause of our death because we might gain enemies and be exposed to robbers and thieves who kill us for our money. Friends and the people around us might also cause our death. So generally, we think that all these different things and people around us are useful to us and make us happy. But we should realize that they also constitute possible causes of our death.

We also shouldn't think that because we are alive now, we can manage to escape death. Death could

IMPERMANENCE

strike at any time. We are not sure when we are going to die because there are so many causes of death. We also can't believe that until we die, we can just take it easy. We do not know when we are going to die, but the only certainty is that we are going to die. In the past there have been many great kings and they have had to die. There have been great soldiers and people with much courage and they've had to die. There have been very wealthy people, but they have also had to die. So the kings couldn't give orders to stop death, brave soldiers couldn't avoid their death with their bravery, and wealthy people couldn't find any way of buying their way out of death. There is just no way of escaping death. Once we realize that, we shouldn't just ignore the thought. We cannot afford to discard the understanding of impermanence. Once we are aware of it, then we must see what we can do to face death without fear. We must find what we can do so we will be prepared to face death properly and positively.

Spending all our time speculating on the future and making plans is a total waste of time because we are not doing anything to prepare ourselves for death that might come at any time. It is more important to practice the dharma than to make plans. Imagine making plans for next year. We don't know what is going to come first, the plans or our death. If death comes before the year is up, our plans have been wasted. If we are not dead before the year, then it will help a little bit. But had we begun to practice the dharma and generate as much virtue as we could during that time; then whether we die or don't our time was not wasted. It is more important to practice the dharma than to engage in any other activity. Meditating on impermanence and on the possibility of death will stimulate our practice so that we can do what is good for us, because we'll be free from the fear of death and eventually achieve the fruition of our practice and be of great help to other beings. Simply thinking that impermanence generates suffering and not doing anything about it is not going to help us, and it is not going to help other beings either. So impermanence can prompt us to act in a positive way for ourselves and for other beings. So this is why it is useful to meditate on impermanence and the many causes of death.

The fourth way to meditate on impermanence is to think of what happens at the time of death. Meditating on this should really stimulate our wish to practice. What happens at the time of death? For the most part it is a painful experience, and this is why most people do not want to think about it. But it is quite foolish to ignore it because we are going to have to experience it. We all have to face death so it's quite pointless to want to forget about it. It is far better to try to prepare ourselves for it.

We can see what happens to other people when they die, the kinds of hallucinations that they go through. This happens to everyone and is going to happen to us as well. We shouldn't think that people don't mind death, because nobody wants to die. This is why we have to prepare ourselves through the

---

[11] When one dies, the mind goes into the *bardo* which is an intermediate place between life and death. There one encounters horrifying visions which are described in the *Tibetan Book of the Dead*.

IMPERMANENCE

practice of dharma. When the day of our death comes, most likely we won't think, "Oh well, it's okay. Today is the day of my death. I'm dying. I don't mind." Most people aren't happy about dying. So when the time of death comes, if we have been prepared through the practice of dharma, we will be able to face it positively, without fear.

The fifth way to meditate on impermanence is to think about what happens after we've died. If we think about impermanence in this way, we will realize that this life is really very meaningless. This thought will really reduce our clinging to the things of this life. Even if we are extremely rich, once we are dead, everything has to be left behind. We can't take even one penny with us. Even if we have great stores of food, we can't take one bit of food with us. Even if we have lots of friends, we can't take even one of them with us. We can't even take our body with us. The only thing that survives death is our consciousness. Our consciousness goes all by itself, and at that point nothing else is of any benefit to us. Whether we were rich or poor, unknown or famous, beautiful or ugly; nothing makes any difference when we die. Our consciousness just goes all by itself. All that helps us at death is whatever practice of the dharma we were able to do in our lifetime to develop the quality of meditation in us. If we have this, it will help us at death and we will have no fear or pain.

If we can use these five ways of meditating on impermanence, they will greatly increase our wish to practice and our interest in the dharma. Also they will encourage us to eliminate our unwholesome behavior. We will find that our tendency to become drowsy or agitated in meditation will be greatly reduced and all of this will result in a stronger wish to practice.

When we meditate on impermanence, our practice will improve automatically and our negative aspects will decrease. The Buddha said that among all the various meditations, this is really the highest, best meditation. If a robber were to come and you were not aware of it, he might just enter and kill you for your possessions. If, however, you knew that the robber was coming, you could prepare yourself by leaving or hiding. You might still have some fear of the robber, but you wouldn't be in such a great danger and you could protect yourself. If you meditate on impermanence and are aware that death is certain, it will be very helpful to you. So when we use the instructions of the Buddha and realize that death will come, we can be prepared for it, and when it comes, there won't be any major difficulties.

Summary

We are very fortunate to have a very precious human birth. Once we have something so precious, every instant of time during this life is precious. So we mustn't waste it, and this is very important. We meditate on impermanence to become aware of the need not to waste time. If this human existence of ours was just very ordinary, only filled with trouble and pain

IMPERMANENCE

with no hope of ever finding any happiness, then maybe we would think in the same way as somebody who has been thrown in prison—just counting the days. With the one year sentence, one day goes by and we think, "Oh, that's great, it's one day less." When a month has gone by we think, "Oh, fantastic, only eleven more months to go." When two months have gone by, we really rejoice. We may think like this in an extremely bad situation; but we are in an extremely fortunate situation. We have a precious human existence which gives us the possibility of realizing Buddhahood. It's a very, very rare thing and it's very useful for oneself and for other beings. So while we have it, we should get out of it all that we can because it won't last forever. But while we have it, we have to make the best of it. This is why we have to meditate on impermanence.

We might think that meditating on impermanence might be dangerous, because it is a very unpleasant subject to meditate on. But this isn't so because impermanence isn't likely to dominate one's mind. If problems in life arise, they bring mental troubles anyway; but meditation on impermanence itself is not likely to cause any damage. On the contrary, it's extremely positive because through this meditation we learn how to recognize this intrinsic feature of phenomena. Having learned how everything is changing, we learn how to cope with this impermanence. Once we have learned that everything is impermanent, we don't become completely frozen in fear and become more and more afraid. On the contrary, facing impermanence means using whatever time we have in the best possible way. If we use this time properly, there is no need to fear anything. Meditating on impermanence makes us become very aware of the passing of time and stimulates our diligence and efficiency in what we are doing. We are able to do a lot more and are able to apply ourselves better to what is virtuous. We are also able to develop much better meditation. We feel very fulfilled, very happy, because we have been able to do a lot of good things. So meditation on impermanence doesn't depress us. On the contrary, it makes us very happy, because we have been able to use our time very positively.

From the time the Buddha gave this teaching on impermanence until now, this teaching has helped many beings tremendously. The Buddha gave the teaching on impermanence, and after him all the great teachers of the hīnayāna, the mahāyāna, and the vajrayāna have used this teaching. They have meditated on impermanence in order to turn their own mind to the dharma and to stimulate their diligence in their practice. So when we don't reflect very much on it, we may think that impermanence is a rather gloomy subject. But under a more careful analysis, we will realize how beneficial it is.

The Third Reminder:

Karma

(Tib. *le gyundre*)

Accept (what is positive) and reject (what is negative)

CHAPTER 3

Karma

Although we might occasionally be able to act in a positive, wholesome manner, we won't be able to keep this up for very long if we haven't really turned our mind to the dharma. To turn our mind to the dharma, we need to meditate on the four ways of turning the mind away from saṃsara.

We have already studied two of the four topics. The first was a precious human birth endowed with all the freedoms and assets, and the second was death and impermanence. The third topic, karma, explains the connection between our actions and the effects of these actions. The Buddha has said that this topic is very difficult to understand. It is very difficult to understand because if we look at our present actions, we don't immediately see the effects of them. Also, if we see the effects of our actions, we do not see the actions which gave rise to this result. This makes it difficult to believe in the causality of our actions.

To understand karma, we need to understand why things are impermanent and empty.[12] The subject of causality of actions is very subtle, because the connection between our actions and their consequences are very difficult to prove. Only buddhas and bodhisattvas can see this connection directly. However, closer examination allows us to understand something about this causality of our actions.

The word "karma" in the West is used in a very wide sense to mean a connection between our actions and their consequences, although etymologically "karma" only means "action." In this chapter, however, we will use the word "karma" in the wide sense of actions and their results.

Some persons believe that there is no law of karma and that whatever they do will not bring about any specific consequences. They do not believe that good actions will bring good results and that bad actions will bring about unpleasant and painful results. Some religions don't believe in karma, but Buddhist do. Since it is a very subtle topic, it is hard to decide who is right and who is wrong. This is why we have to look at the reasons for each position and then perhaps we can identify which is correct.

First of all, those who do not believe in karma say that there is no such thing as karma because one cannot see the connection between our actions and their results directly. These people believe that whatever

---

[12] By empty (Skt. *śūnyatā*) we do not mean empty like an empty glass, but empty as in empty of inherent existence.

happiness human beings enjoy is due entirely to their own efforts. They believe, for instance, that if we are wealthy and enjoying a good position in life, it is just the result of their own hard work. But not seeing something doesn't really prove anything, because if we do not see something, it does not necessarily prove that it does not exist. For example, we all have thoughts running through our minds all the time, but no one else sees these thoughts. So if someone were to say, "There are no such things as thoughts because I cannot see them," that would be incorrect reasoning. So not seeing the result of karma is not a valid reason to say there is no karma.

Taking another example, imagine someone dreaming. Looking at this person, we can't see the dream the person is having. But we cannot then say, "He is not dreaming because I don't see it." As far as that person is concerned, he is experiencing a dream, and our not seeing the dream does not disprove his experience of the dream. So to say that karma or past lives are not true because one cannot see them is also not a valid reason for disproving karma or past lives.

The argument of those who believe in karma runs like this: We can see that there are many different kinds of people—some are born in the East, some in the West. All these different people have very different experiences. Some are born in a place with a favorable environment such as a place of wealth where living is easy and people are well educated. Then some are born in very impoverished areas where there is not enough food and living is hard.

What is the reason behind these differences? Is it something that comes from their own choice? Are they born in an impoverished place because they choose where they were born? Well, if they chose their birth then everyone would think, "I want to be born in a place where everything is easy, where the living is good, and where I can be rich and happy." Then there wouldn't be people who would choose to be born in a difficult place with problems and suffering. So it is quite clear that one is born in a difficult environment not out of choice.

The reason for these differences of birth is to be found in the consequences of our actions in a past lifetime. The quality of our actions in the past will determine the environment we will be born in. For instance, some people will be born in a place in which they have much happiness and some will be born in very difficult conditions. Some will be born in a very good social environment, some will be born in a very bad one. Some will be rich, some poor. All of this is determined by our previous actions.

When we talk about karma, this relationship between our previous actions and what is happening to us now, we might think that this is terrible because our bad actions create suffering and good actions bring about happiness. We might think that this is really quite a depressing prospect, since we might have to suffer a lot because of what we did or because of what we were unable to do. But what we have to understand is that karma doesn't mean that we have to suffer passively with whatever is happening. On the contrary, it means that we have a very great amount of choice in determining what kind of life we want for ourselves in the future. We have the possibility to create our own happiness and to eliminate our suffering. It is entirely up to us to decide how we want to act; we can create the good consequences we want and eliminate the bad consequences that we don't want.

When we study karma, we will see how we can create the causal conditions for happiness, which are virtuous actions, and get rid of the causal conditions of suffering, which are unvirtuous actions. The first chapter explained the eight freedoms and ten assets. The next chapter described the various aspects of impermanence. In this present chapter there are two main parts: illustrating what are virtuous actions and what are unvirtuous actions. We will learn to identify these two aspects and discover that there are ten unvirtuous things to be eliminated and what virtuous actions are to be cultivated. The ten unvirtuous actions are classified as either physical, verbal, or mental.

The Unvirtuous Actions of Body

The first unvirtuous action is killing. When one talks about killing, there should be the intention to kill. Killing that is accidental or didn't have the intention to kill is not a unvirtuous action. For instance, a doctor operating on a person or giving him a strong medicine which he thinks will help the patient and the patient dies as a result of the operation or the medicine, this is not the unvirtuous act of killing. Second, if one just thinks, "I want to kill this person," without actually doing the killing, it is not the unvirtuous act of killing. So for this to be a unvirtuous action, not only does one have to think "I want to kill," but one actually has to go though with killing the person.

There are three types of killing based on one's motivation. The first is killing because of desire, which is trying to kill a person or animal to gain something for oneself or material profit. The second type is killing because of aggression. One thinks one has an enemy even if it's an animal, and one thinks that one is being harmed by this enemy or by this animal. One wants to get rid of the person or animal and kill it. This can be done with either weapons or poison, but one gets rid of the person out of strong anger. The third type of killing is rooted in ignorance. It is when someone believes that killing is all right or even good and just doesn't know how bad killing is. So they kill because they do not understand the wrong they are doing such as sacrificing an animal.

It is indeed very bad to commit the negative action of killing. If one kills another person, one is depriving this person of his life and whatever enjoyment he or she had. One is forcing this person to face the fear and the pain of death, so indeed it is very wrong to do. There are three kinds of consequences that a killer will have as a result of killing. The first consequence of the ripening of this karma is that he or she will have to endure a very painful consequence in his next lifetime and most likely have a very unpleasant birth. The second consequence of karma is that the result will be similar to the act done. So the result for a killer is that since he shortened the lifetime of another, he will most likely have a very short lifetime himself. A third consequence or karmic result is that in the next lifetime, there will be a propensity for the person to act in the same way again so that this person will have a natural tendency to enjoy killing or want to kill.

The antidote for this killing is the virtue of abstaining from killing. If one doesn't kill, then one will not have to go through the very painful consequence of killing. One will also be much better off in the next lifetime as well as this lifetime. The Buddha said that one does not have to give up what is beneficial (as one does in asceticism), but has to give up only what is harmful because it causes pain and suffering. Killing is just like this. If one kills someone, one won't derive anything good from it in this lifetime because, for instance, the friends of the person killed may take their revenge. So all the time one lives in fear of revenge and one also might be sent to prison. So not giving up killing not only creates very much suffering in the future, but it creates a great deal of trouble in the present. Even in the short-term, refraining from killing frees one from all the fears and problems that would come with killing. So not killing automatically gives one a lot of peace, a lot of goodness that one wouldn't enjoy if one had killed.

In view of this, we should resolve that from now until we die, we are not going to do any killing. It is really essential to avoid killing. If we stop, from this virtue we will gather a great deal of positive spiritual energy. The results for the next lifetime may be that we will most likely have a long lifetime and be free from sickness.

The Buddha said in the *Prātimokṣa* sūtra that one should give up all unwholesome actions and cultivate virtuous ones. This advice doesn't mean that one has to give up everything that is pleasant, good, or nice and cultivate everything that is difficult, painful, and unpleasant. If one looks at it closely, one will see that what one has to give up is not happiness, but something dreadful, like a poison. It is the cause of all suffering in this lifetime and the next. So if one can manage to eliminate it, one will eliminate the very ground of suffering. It will be like being freed from fetters. Instead of seeing it as something difficult, it leads one to the end of difficulty and pain.

The second negative action of the body is stealing. If one does not give up stealing, it will be a cause of great harm to others and oneself. If someone is rich or even if he doesn't own very much, they are very attached and involved with what they own. A rich man likes his wealth; a poor man likes whatever ordinary objects he possesses because he probably went through a lot of effort to acquire what he has. In the end they are able to obtain it and once they have it, it becomes as valuable as their own heart. And if someone comes along and steals this or if it's taken from them by force, it brings them great suffering. So stealing generates a great deal of mental pain and may also cause others the suffering of poverty after losing what they own.

Stealing brings a lot of unhappiness to other people, but it also brings difficulties to the one who is stealing. To steal, one first knows that someone has something that they want and one covets this. Then one goes through difficulties to take this thing, and this might also be difficult physically and mentally to do. Finally, once one has acquired it, one will be in fear of being punished for what one has done. Furthermore, because desire is something that can never be satisfied, because craving gets stronger, once one has stolen, then one will feel the urge to do it again. Then this does not satisfy one completely and one keeps on because one never feels one has enough. Even if continual stealing endangers one's life, one still goes on until the end when one is in a lot of trouble. So stealing brings unhappiness and pain to other beings and also for oneself.

The Buddha said stealing is a cause of unhappiness and is like a poison. Stealing isn't very pleasant and the Buddha has said, "You know it's not good, you have to give it up." That is what stealing really is: a cause of great pain for others and for oneself. This is true for this lifetime and it is also true for the next lifetime, because when the karma of stealing ripens in the next lifetime, it will create great suffering for oneself. If one can give up stealing, then it will bring peace and happiness to others and oneself. As the

Buddha himself said, "The dharma is peace; it is freedom from craving."

There are three kinds of theft. The first kind is stealing by force such as a strong person directly attacking another person and taking his or her possessions. This also happens during a war when the possessions of the vanquished are taken. The second type of theft is robbery, which is stealing when the victim isn't there. The third type of stealing is by deceit such as using false weights or measures or pretending something is very precious and charging a high price when it is actually very cheap material.

There are a number of things that are not really counted as stealing. First, if one takes something of very little value, which is very unimportant and thinks, "Oh, that won't make any difference." Secondly, if one has a very close friend and takes something that belongs to that friend. Third, if one takes something that is very harmful. For example, if somebody has poison and one takes this poison and hides it. If this is done for a good motivation, then it is not included as stealing.

Giving up stealing is one of the roots of dharma practice. Giving up stealing will be a source of great happiness, because it means that there won't be any major difficulty interrupting one's practice. One won't be beset by the fears that are a part of stealing and others won't have to live in fear of us. One won't have to fear anything, so the other people will be more like friends to one. So that leaves a very good mental space for practice without any problems. This is why it is said that if one can give up stealing, it is a most excellent part of the practice.

The third negative physical action is inappropriate sexual relationships which, in this context, means adultery. The Buddha has said adultery is bad and something to avoid because it generates much pain for a lot of people. So in one's own interest and in the interest of other people, it is very important to try to give it up. It will bring more peace and more happiness to others and to oneself. What is meant exactly by adultery? Adultery is when two people are living together in harmony, love each other, and someone separates them through seducing one of them. This will create very much pain and unhappiness between the couple who were united. Adultery is also a situation which is likely to generate many problems and be hard on all sides. It will be hard for the couple that splits up, and it will be hard for the seducer. So if one refrains from adultery, there will be no hardship of any kind involved. One will be able to have a nice relationship with people without any problems, and one will be able to be relaxed and loving without any other difficulty.

There are three kinds of inappropriate sexual relationships. The first kind is with those protected by family which means one shouldn't have any relationship with someone who is part of the same family as one (incest). The second type is with those who are protected by the dharma, meaning having sexual relations with those who have taken the monastic vows. The third type is with those who are protected by their parents, young people who are still living with their parents. It is wrong to have sexual relationships with such persons because it will bring much suffering to the parents. To give up improper sexual relationships automatically frees one from a great source of difficulty and pain and any legal risk.

The result of having proper sexual relations is that the mind will be happier. There will be a greater feeling of ease and one will feel more in control of one's mind. This will also be good for one's practice because when meditating, one won't be distracted by so many different thoughts. It is said that the nature of happiness is to be at peace, and giving up wrong sexual relationships will bring one peace. This will cause an easier life this time and in the next lifetime because carrying on wrong sexual relationships in this lifetime will probably result in a painful rebirth in one of the three lower realms (animal, hungry ghost, or hell realms). Also, if one becomes used to a wrong sexual practice in this lifetime, then the habit will still be with one in the next lifetime, continuing suffering. If one is able to give it up in this lifetime, then one will develop the habit of pure conduct, and this will grow and be with one continuously so that one's mind will truly be able to turn to the dharma and one's practice will really be part of the path of dharma.

Actions of Speech

There are four unvirtuous verbal actions. The first of these is telling lies. Telling lies is a source of difficulties for everyone. It might seem that while one is telling a lie, it may be very pleasant to do and save some trouble. But in fact lying generates trouble and pain very quickly. If one can give up lying, it will bring about peace and happiness. One may ask, who is the person we lie to? It isn't the people who do not trust us, because whatever we say wouldn't be believed anyway. We usually lie to people who trust and like us. We feel we can deceive them, so we lie to make them believe something which is not true. If they believe it, it is likely to bring many difficulties later on. While we are lying we think, "Well, I've really managed to put one over on them." But it says in the teachings that the one who is lying is the one really fooled. The only person really deceived is the liar himself, because the other people are not fooled. They learn that the person is not capable of speaking truthfully. They will always think when the liar comes along that he is going to try to deceive them, so they aren't deceived.

The second unvirtuous action of speech is slander. This is speech which promotes one's own interests and hurts others. One also uses this slander to divide people. If one knows people who are good friends and to promote one's own interests or to cause them pain or suffering, one says something out of anger or stupidity that will have a very painful effect on them or cause disharmony; this is slander.

Such slander is very harmful because, to begin with, if there are two persons who trust each other, who try to help each other and to enjoy each other's company, they will have a feeling of love between them which is positive. If one slanders them trying to split them up, instead of this love and compassion it will bring about mistrust, anger, resentment, pride, jealously and so on causing disharmony. In the short-term a bad action will bring much suffering to both parties. In the long-term these people may develop a very strong ill will towards each other and may do many negative actions causing much future suffering. So all of this immediate suffering and future suffering will be due to one bad action.

This divisive slander is not only painful for the victims but will also bring many bad results for the one who is slandering. People will get to know about the slander and talk to each other, and learn that the person is a bad person. So one will not find it easy to have friends and will develop a lot of enemies causing much pain in this lifetime. It will also cause much suffering in the next lifetime, because slandering will cause thoughts of aggression and resentment and then in the next lifetime one will have a propensity to fight, be jealous and angry and cause many harmful deeds and, in turn, much suffering.

If one does not slander, then one will not create any division among people who like each other. Usually, one slanders not against enemies because they are already divided, but against those who are close, who love each other and have a positive relationship. So not to slander means that these good relationships between people will not be broken up, and one will be in a position to have better relationships with other people. One will benefit from this because one will be able to have better friends and fewer enemies. So the result will be good for this lifetime and for the next lifetime, since one won't have accumulated negative tendencies for the next lifetime.

The third negative action of speech is harsh speech or harmful words. This is speaking out of anger or other negative feelings with the intention to hurt others. One might think that harsh words are not actually causing any physical pain to others, such as causing sickness or making them feel hungry or thirsty. So why is it bad? In fact, these harmful words are as dangerous as weapons because when one speaks to another person in a harsh way, it generates a very great deal of mental pain which could trigger anger or other negative feelings. So in the end the the other person one has had harsh words with may feel that they can't be in the same place as us.

So this kind of harsh speech is very painful, and there is nothing to be gained except trouble from it. At first it might be a great relief to be able to just say a few harsh words to someone, but nothing will be accomplished because one is going to stir up similar feelings in the other person. And this will go back and forth and will generate a great deal of pain for the other person and will also rebound in one's own mind.

It's very valuable to give up harmful speech because it will decrease one's anger and one's negative motivations will decrease a great deal. One will also be able to gain some more positive motivation towards others. Then one will be able to make friends with others much better. With a good disposition, one will be able to make friends and gain more peace and happiness. It's really worth making effort even on a very small scale. Every time one has the feeling one is going to say harsh words, if one can stop even one word, it is very beneficial.

The fourth negative action of speech is useless chatter. This is speaking without a purpose or what might be called "idle gossip."

Summary

When we receive teachings, we should put our mind into the disposition of enlightenment. This is called the "precious mind of enlightenment" or "the precious *bodhicitta*." If we have this motivation, whatever virtuous act we do becomes very great and leads us to the point where we can eliminate suffering forever. So at all times it is very important to try to make sure that we have pure motivation so that whatever actions we do are not wasted and are really bringing us toward enlightenment. The way we can determine the purity of our motivation is to turn our mind inwards and examine ourselves. We should all the time try to determine if what we are doing is inspired by pure or impure motivation. Because we have had a long habit of having negative motivations, we will have to modify our behavior artificially. To do this we have to look at our motivation each time and try to improve it little by little until it becomes a more natural process and our motivation naturally becomes clearer and clearer. So it is important to never forget that the reason we are receiving teachings is to achieve Buddhahood in order to help all other beings. Until now what we have done to help beings has been very limited, so we should want to achieve Buddhahood for the sake of all beings. To achieve Buddhahood, of course, we must practice the dharma and to practice we must, of course, recei teachings.

There are many reasons why we need to practice the four ordinary foundations. First of all, we need to turn our mind to the dharma. We need to be able to practice dharma in this lifetime, and this is why we meditate on a precious human life. If we don't use it now, then maybe we won't find the same opportunity again in another time. We may believe that there is plenty of time to practice and take it easy and very slowly. But if we do that, we will fall under the power of idleness and because this lifetime is not permanent; our life may end before we know it and our opportunity will have been wasted. This is why we need to meditate on the second point of impermanence.

We meditate on the third point of karma because it tells us how we can practice. When we study karma, we learn that we should practice virtuous actions and give up unvirtuous actions. But we also should realize that we are not aiming for just a very limited form of happiness. We don't want temporary relief from pain, and we shouldn't think that the present pain is greater than the pain we might experience in the future. What we have to realize is that the person in the future experiencing the pain will still be ourselves, and the suffering later will be no different from the pain now. So we shouldn't think in the short-term but aim at changeless happiness. We should aim at the definite, irreversible liberation from suffering so that we never have to suffer again.

The Fourth Reminder:

The Faults of Saṃsāra

(Tib. *kor way nye mik*)

The Fourth Reminder:

The Faults of Saṃsāra

(Tib. *kor wa'i nye dmik*)

(Remember saṃsāra is) impermanent

CHAPTER 4
The Faults of Saṃsāra

The fourth ordinary foundation is the the faults of conditioned existence (Skt. *saṃsāra*). The suffering in conditioned existence is usually described in terms of suffering of the six types of beings who live in saṃsāra. This usually poses a problem for a number of people because they can't directly see some of these realms such as the hell or hungry ghost realm. Because they can't be seen, one might have doubts and begin to ask if there are really such realms, and do these beings really undergo such terrible suffering. We have to understand that these realms do exist, and they exist because people form mental habits which create these realms. Let us take an example. If someone is sleeping and others look at him or her, they see someone sleeping. They see a body lying there, not moving and they cannot see the person's mind. That person might be experiencing being in a beautiful place with wonderful persons, or that person could be dreaming of a horrible experience such as being imprisoned or being attacked by wild animals. From the outside we can't tell what the person is experiencing. Now the type of experiences that are going on in a person's mind are determined by the person's mental imprints from earlier experiences. So if the person has had a lot of negative experiences in the past, he or she is likely to have very frightful and painful dreams. If a person has learned to let his mind be more relaxed and peaceful in the past, then he will probably have very good and pleasant experiences in his dreams.

In the short-term we can see how the various mental habits of a person create the different types of experiences in a dream. This works also in the long-term so that when someone has developed certain kinds of mental habits or patterns in this lifetime, it will affect experiences at death. When a person dies, all we see on the outside is a corpse which is very much like observing someone who is asleep. There is a body which is not moving and we do not see what that person's experiences are. But the mind of that person is having all kinds of experiences which are determined by the positive and negative actions that the person did in his or her previous lifetime.

The Three Lower Realms

Negative actions that we commit will cause some very frightful and painful experiences. So those who have had very strong hatred and anger and have killed or committed very serious sexual offenses will end up experiencing the terrible suffering of the hell realm. The reason is that those under the influence of anger and hatred with the wish to harm others develop such a strong mental habit that it will result in the effect of experiencing the suffering of the hell realms as unbearable heat or unbearable cold. Because the mind has become so used to anger and hatred, the mind will think of fighting other persons, of killing and harming them with different weapons, and think of ways to make them suffer. At death all these thoughts will be experienced by oneself. Because the negative karma that has been gathered is so powerful, then these experiences go on for a very long time and so the experiences of the hell realm go on for a very, very long time.

We should be aware that if we are born in the hell realm, we cannot expect anything but constant suffering. We already have had some little taste of this suffering in our current life when we have had the experience that our suffering is unbearable. Then imagine how it would be to go through this constant terrible agony in the hell realm. Once we realize this, we should really try to avoid this hell realm at all costs. And it is completely up to us. We should do all we can to avoid being born in the hell realm, not only for this lifetime, but forever. We can choose whether we want to stop the possibility of this terrible agony or whether we want to stop forever.

The second form of intense suffering of conditioned existence is the suffering of hungry ghosts who feel starved and very, very thirsty all the time. They have these experiences because of a very great habit of avarice in previous lives. Through avarice these people have never been able to do anything positive and have accumulated a lot of bad karma. The feeling that goes with greed is a feeling of want. One feels that one is going to miss something, that one is going to need something. And when this thought becomes very deeply engraved in the mind, then in the next lifetime it will produce a constant feeling of want, of desire. So these beings constantly have the feeling that they are very hungry and thirsty, and will never find enough food and drink to satisfy them. They will be like very, very poor people without food, clothes, or drink. Again using the example of a dream, we can understand this better. For example, we may lay a lot of jewels and money next to a poor person who is dreaming. Because this person is dreaming about his utter poverty, these jewels cannot benefit him. In the same way, beings who are born as hungry ghosts might be born in our world, but they cannot see or experience the available necessities of life. They cannot experience any satisfaction because of the bad karma which is obscuring their perception and making them perceive a constant lack of food and drink even though these things are actually there. Once we know about this realm of suffering, we should do everything we can in order to avoid such a painful state.

The third lower state of saṃsāra is that of animals. This is much easier to understand because we can see animals. But we don't really conceive of their suffering because we have not really looked at it closely enough to understand just how much suffering they

THE FAULTS OF SAMSĀRA

have. Their first problem is their great stupidity. They do not have an intelligent mind like ours that can decide what is beneficial or not. They cannot use speech in a positive way and are not able to experience true happiness. They are not able to get rid of pain, and if they are domesticated they do not have any choice of how their life goes. They are slaughtered by men and they kill each other. So they are continually undergoing many hardships.

The reason why beings are born as animals is that they have a basic ignorance that comes from not knowing how things work. When this ignorance becomes a very strong habit, then they are born as an animal. Once we know about this realm and what causes rebirth as an animal, we can avoid it. There is no need for us to go through such pains in the next lifetime and the next for hundreds or even thousands of lives. We cannot fall into such a state if we practice the dharma.

We have to remember that in Buddhism there is the very, very important principle of cause and effect. One cannot have an effect unless there is a cause. And conversely, when there is a cause one cannot avoid its effect. Take, for example, a flower. If we say, "I want a flower," no matter how much we want it, unless we have sown a seed earlier, we are not going to get a flower. On the other hand, if we have sown the seed of a flower, whether we want a flower or not, there will be a flower growing from the seed. In the same way, as long as we create the cause of suffering, we are going to have suffering whether we want it or not. And if we want happiness, we are not just going to find it. If we want happiness, we have to create the cause of happiness, which is virtue. If we don't want suffering, there is no point saying "I don't want it." The point is to abandon the cause of suffering, which is negative actions. So once we understand this, we can practice accordingly and stop creating more suffering and find happiness.

The Three Higher Realms

The three higher realms are called the "higher realms" because beings who are in these realms are gods, or jealous gods, and human beings. They go through the same excruciating pains as beings in the lower states of existence. They have some good karma, but also some karma tainted by the presence of defilements. Because they have good but tainted karma, these beings have a better physical form than the beings in the three lower realms. Also their minds are intelligent and they have the capacity to apply themselves diligently to various tasks. But these beings are still subject to the law of composites[13] or conditioned existence. They are still affected by defilements, which means that they are still within the sphere of suffering. Anyone who lives in saṃsāra, even in the higher states, still has suffering. Suffering

[13] This is the law that everything made of other parts (composites) will eventually fall apart. For example, the body is made of elements and eventually (after death) it will return to being elements.

THE FAULTS OF SAMSĀRA

is there all the time. Even if it's not present in an acute form, the potential of suffering is always there. This is why we are trying to achieve Buddhahood. Even though we may have some happiness at the moment, this is not lasting.

Beings in the higher realms do not suffer as violently as beings of the lower realms, but they still suffer because they see the possibility of suffering all the time. So even if one is in the higher states, one still has to try to reach complete freedom from suffering (Buddhahood or enlightenment) which is beyond conditioned existence.

The gods are beings who seem to have the best possible happiness. Their whole life is nothing but pleasure and enjoyment. Because they are lost in these pleasures, they do not have any impulse to practice the dharma. Although their life is very pleasant, it doesn't go on for a very long time and soon comes to an end. When it comes to an end, then the gods go through what is known as the "suffering of death and transformation (to a lower birth)." Because gods have some powers of clairvoyance, they all have five types of visions when they are going to die to tell them that they are dying.[14] This is a very painful moment for a god, because he can see that his life of great enjoyment and pleasure is now finished and that he has to go through other realms of existence where, by comparison, there is going to be a lot of suffering.

[14] These visions are things such as flowers wilting, the body smelling, and friends leaving.

If we look at the jealous gods, their happiness and enjoyment is not as plentiful as those of the gods, so they are not quite as involved in their happiness. But they are afflicted by a very, very strong jealously, which is the result of having had that very strong feeling in previous lives. So they feel jealousy of the great happiness of the gods all the time. They are also jealous of the happiness of the other jealous gods. They have this dreadful feeling of jealousy that eats away at them so that even though they have enjoyment, they can't really savor it properly because they are constantly suffering pangs of jealousy. When their jealousy becomes very strong, they begin fighting and feeling a lot of resentment towards each other. Sometimes they even die from fighting with each other. So it is a very painful situation.

Human beings have a different situation from the other realms. They do not have the tremendous pleasures of the gods, which means they do not get so carried away by all these pleasures, and they do not suffer the tremendous pains of the lower states. So the human condition is the very best position to be in to practice the dharma and realize Buddhahood. This is why a human life is called a precious jewel. It is endowed with all the freedoms and assets for practicing the dharma. A human life has the ability and readiness to practice dharma because there aren't too many the pleasures to make one forget to practice and there isn't the unceasing suffering of the three lower realms that is so overwhelming that one cannot practice at all. Unlike animals, human beings have a certain amount of intelligence and are able to be content with what they have and renounce it. So there are a lot of qualities that make it possible to practice and achieve enlightenment.

However, because the human condition is the very best condition for practicing the dharma, it is not also necessarily an extremely happy condition. If one is a human being, one still has to suffer quite a great deal because the human condition is plagued by the four sufferings of birth, sickness, old age, and death.

When we are conceived, it is painful because we do not have a body and have to go through the whole process of acquiring a physical form inside the womb of our mother. When we come out of the womb, it is also painful. Once we are born, we are in a way very stupid. We can't speak, dress, eat, or walk by ourselves and are totally helpless. We need the help of our parents and are not able to understand anything by ourselves. So this is the suffering that goes along with birth.

We may say that later when we grow up things will get better. But even this is not going to last very long because it will be interrupted by either old age or sickness. We shouldn't think that, "Well, maybe I can escape old age or sickness." There is no question of avoiding them. It is certain that at one point or another we will be hit by old age or by sickness. When old age comes, the whole process of degradation sets in so that even if we were very strong before, we become weak. Even if we were very intelligent, our intelligence dwindles and lessens. It is a whole process of change that is very painful and depressing. If we are struck by sickness, then our body becomes nothing but pain that sometimes is unbearable and we wish to do away with it, but we can't; we have to go through the pain. Besides this, when we are aging or sick, there is an added misery, which is the thought of death. We will have this fear that after all we are going to die and this unbearable event will happen. Then at the end we have to go through death, which is very painful because once we are dead, we don't know what's going to happen or where we are going to go.

So when we talk about the precious human birth, we are talking about something which is very precious and useful for dharma practice. The six states of saṃsāra are not taught to frighten people. They are taught so that people can realize that there's a state which is beyond all these various types of sufferings even as a human being. There is a possibility to be rid of all this suffering and there's a possibility of finding true happiness. With practice, the path of dharma can go from one happiness to another, because if one creates the cause of happiness, one reaps the fruit of happiness until one eventually achieves complete happiness.

If one thinks one might still find some happiness by looking for it in money or fame or pleasures, one is mistaken because that type of happiness just doesn't last. It isn't worth clinging to. One should be aiming for happiness that stays forever and which can be achieved only through the proper practice of the dharma.

Summary of the Four Foundations

These four topics that have been examined are called the four ordinary preliminary practices. These are called "ordinary" because they are not special instructions or secret in any way. They are something ordinary in that everybody can see and can understand them and they are visible to everyone. If anyone thinks carefully about impermanence or the suffering of saṃsāra or karma, they can understand it. The same thing is true of the precious human life. So there is nothing very extraordinary or very hidden about these teachings. In contrast, the teachings such as the "thatness" or *dharmatā* of phenomena are only accessible to realized beings.

All the time we see impermanence, we see the sufferings of saṃsāra. We see it, we know it, but we don't remember. We think, "All right, saṃsāra is suffering, but maybe next month it is going to get a bit better. If it doesn't get better next month, then maybe next year." So all the time we keep entertaining some kind of hope even though we know that saṃsāra's suffering occurs continually. We are always hoping for something a bit better inside it. So although we know, we don't really acknowledge what we know. The same thing is true for impermanence. We know that everything is impermanent, but we still hold onto the idea of things being eternal. We still believe that things are going to go on just as they are now and still make the mistake of not really thinking of change. So the whole point of these meditations is to make us see clearly what exists and to make us recognize what we see. If we can see them really clearly, then our mind will turn to the dharma automatically. So the point is not just to see all these things but to really recognize them, and having recognized them, translate them into action.

The reason why these practices are called the preliminary practices is because they come before we can do the actual practice. We have to have a certain amount of preparation. Some teachers say that the preliminary practices are even more important than the actual practice. And in a way, this is true because it depends entirely on the preliminary practices as to whether we can turn our mind to the dharma or not, whether we can really recognize things properly and trust the truth that is pointed out in these teachings. All this depends entirely on the practice of the preliminary teachings.

Suffering is an inherent feature of saṃsāra, so each of us has problems and troubles of our own. Sometimes we may think, "Well, this is what's wrong with me. This is my particular pain. This is my problem." But we have to realize that these problems are shared by all other beings. Everyone who lives in saṃsāra has suffering because this is the intrinsic feature of saṃsāra. So when we have troubles or difficulties, we might do things that relieve these difficulties temporarily or we might try different ways to escape the problem or to relieve the pain; but the solution from this will not be very long lasting. Soon the difficulties will be back with the pain because it is inherent to our conditioned existence. And this is true for all other beings as well.

So if we want to go beyond suffering, we mustn't just try to clear it away in the short-term. We mustn't just try to get just a bit better. We must work on the very long-term by using the dharma because the dharma is true, it points out the nature of things, and it can help us immediately. It can help us be happier now, and it will definitely help us find more and more happiness from lifetime to lifetime until we don't have to suffer any more.

So if you wonder how to avoid suffering, don't look for it in specific remedies, but look for it in the dharma because this will certainly take you beyond suffering. This is why the teaching on the four ways of changing the mind, the four ordinary preliminary practices, is given to us.

The Glossary

animal realm See six realms of saṃsāra.

arhat (Tib. *dra chom pa*) Accomplished hīnayāna practitioners who have eliminated the kleśa obscurations. They are the fully realized śrāvakas and pratyekabuddhas.

assets, ten or ten endowments (Skt. *daśasaṁpada*, Tib. *jor wa chu*) These are the factors conducive to practice the dharma. They are being human, being born in a Buddhist place, having sound senses, being free from extreme evil, having faith in the dharma, a buddha having appeared, a buddha having taught, the flourishing of his teachings, people following the teachings, and having compassion towards others.

Avalokiteśvara (Tib. *Chenrezig*) Deity of compassion. He is known as patron deity of Tibet and his mantra is OṂ MAṆI PADME HŪṂ.

bardo (Tib.) Literally, bardo means "between the two." There are six kinds of bardos, but here it refers to the time between death and a rebirth in a new body.

bodhicitta (Tib. *chang chup sem*) Literally, the mind of enlightenment. There are two kinds of bodhicitta: absolute bodhicitta which is completely awakened mind that sees the emptiness of phenomena, and relative bodhicitta which is the aspiration to practice the six pāramitās and free all beings from the sufferings of saṃsāra.

bodhisattva (Tib. *chang chup sem pa*) Literally, one who exhibits the mind of enlightenment; also, an individual who has committed him or herself to the mahāyanā path of compassion and the practice of the six pāramitās to free beings from samsāra.

bodhisattva vow A vow in which one promises to practice in order to bring all other sentient beings to Buddhahood.

Buddha Śākyamuni (Tib. *shakya tubpa*) The Śākyamuni Buddha, often called the Gautama Buddha, refers to the latest Buddha who lived between 563 and 483 B. C.

conditioned existence (Skt. *saṃsāra*, Tib. *kor wa*) Ordinary existence which contains suffering because one still possesses attachment, aggression, and ignorance. It is contrasted to liberation or nirvāṇa.

dharma (Tib. *chö*) This has two main meanings: First it refers to any truth, such as the sky is blue. Second and as used in this text, it refers to the teachings of the Buddha.

dharmatā (Tib. *chö nyi*) Dharmatā is often translated as "suchness" or "the true nature of things," or "things as-they-are." It is phenomena as seen by a completely enlightened being without any distortion or obscuration.

dharmachakra (Skt. for "wheel of dharma," Tib. *chö chi khor lo*) The Buddha's teachings correspond to three levels: the hīnayāna, the mahāyāna and the vajrayāna with each set being one turning of the wheel of dharma.

THE GLOSSARY

eight freedoms (Skt. *aṣṭakṣaṇa*, Tib. *tel wa gye*). These are not living in hell realm, not living in the hungry ghost realm, not living in animal realm, not a long-living god, not having wrong views, not being born in a country without dharma, being mute, or being born in an age without buddhas.

emptiness (Sk. *śūnyatā* Tib. *tong pa nyi*) Also translated as voidness. The Buddha taught in the second turning of the wheel of dharma that external phenomena and the internal phenomena or concept of self or "I" have no real existence and therefore are "empty."

five actions of immediate result These are actions which, if committed, will lead to being immediately reborn in the lower realms. They are killing one's father, killing one's mother, killing an arhat, intentionally wounding a bodhisattva, and dividing the saṅgha.

five poisons (Skt. *kleśas*, Tib. *nyön mong*) The emotional obscurations (in contrast to intellectual obscurations) which are also translated as "poisons." The three main kleśas are (passion or desire or attachment), (aggression or anger) and (ignorance or delusion or aversion). The five kleśas are the three above plus pride and (envy or jealousy).

four ordinary foundations (Tib. *tün mong gi ngon dro shi*) This is meditation on the four thoughts that turn the mind towards the dharma. They are reflection on precious human birth, impermanence and the inevitability of death, karma and its effects, and the pervasiveness of suffering in saṃsāra. In the

mahāmudrā these are called the ordinary foundations.
four thoughts that turn the mind (Tib. *lo dok namshi*) These are realizing the preciousness of human birth, the impermanence of life and inevitability of death, realizing that pleasure and suffering result from good and bad actions, and pervasiveness of the suffering in saṃsāra. They are the same as the four ordinary foundations.
Gampopa (1079-1153 A. D.) One of the main lineage holders of the Kagyu lineage in Tibet. Known also for writing the *Jewel Ornament of Liberation*.
god realms See six realms of saṃsāra.
hell realms See six realms of saṃsāra.
hīnayāna (Tib. *tek pa chung wa*) Literally, the "lesser vehicle." The term refers to the first teachings of the Buddha which emphasized the careful examination of mind and its confusion. Also known as the Theravādin path.
hungry ghosts (Skt. *preta*, Tib. *yidak*) A type of being who is always starved for food and water. See the six realms of saṃsāra.
jealous gods (Skt. *asura*, Tib. *lha ma yin*) See six realms of saṃsāra.
Kagyu (Tib.) One of the four major schools of Buddhism in Tibet. It was founded by Marpa and is headed by His Holiness Karmapa. The other three are the Nyingma, the Sakya, and the Gelupa schools.
kalpa (Skt. *yuga*) An eon lasting several million years.
karma (Tib. *lay*) Literally "action." Karma is a universal law that when one does a wholesome action one's

circumstances will improve and when one does an unwholesome action negative results will eventually occur from the act.
lama (Skt. *guru*) A high teacher in the Tibetan tradition.
mahāmudrā (Tib. *cha ja chen po*) Literally means "great seal" or "great symbol." This meditative transmission emphasizes perceiving mind directly rather than through skillful means.
mahāsiddha (Tib. *drup thop chen po*) A practitioner who has a great deal of realization.
mahāyāna (Tib. *tek pa chen po*) Literally, the "great vehicle." These are the teachings of the second turning of the wheel of dharma, which emphasize śūnyatā, compassion, and universal buddha nature.
ngöndro (Tib. and pronounced "nundro") Tibetan for preliminary practice. One usually begins the vajrayāna path by doing the four preliminary practices which involve about 100,000 refuge prayers and prostrations, 100,000 vajrasattva mantras, 100,000 maṇḍala offerings, and 100,000 guru yoga practices.
Padmasambhava (Tib. *Guru Rinpoche*) He was invited to Tibet in the ninth century A. D. and is known for pacifying the nonBuddhist forces and founding the Nyingma lineage.
path, Buddhist (Tib. *lam*) The path refers to the process of attaining enlightenment. Path may also refer to part of the threefold logic of ground, path, and fruition.
prātimokṣa vows (Tib. *so sor tar pa*) The vows of not killing, stealing, lying, etc. which are taken by monks

and nuns.

pratyekabuddha (Skt., Tib. *rang sang gye*) Literally, solitary realizer. A realized hīnayāna practitioner who has achieved the knowledge of how it is and variety, but who has not committed him or herself to the bodhisattva path of helping all others.

preliminary practices (Tib. *ngöndro)* The four preliminary practices which are done before doing yidam meditation. See ngöndro.

preta Sanskrit for hungry ghosts (see six realms of saṃsāra.

saṃsāra (Tib. *kor wa*) Conditioned existence of ordinary life in which suffering occurs because one still possesses passion, aggression, and ignorance. It is contrasted to nirvāṇa.

saṅgha (Tib. *gendün)*These are the companions on the path. They may be all the persons on the path or the noble saṅgha, which are the realized ones.

six realms of saṃsāra (Tib. *rikdruk*) These are the possible types of rebirths for beings in saṃsāra and are: the god realm in which gods have great pride, the asura realm in which the jealous gods try to maintain what they have, the human realm which is the best realm because one has the possiblity of achieving enlightenment, the animal realm characterized by stupidity, the hungry ghost realm characterized by great craving, and the hell realm characterized by aggression.

śrāvaka (Tib. *nyen thö*) Literally "those who hear" meaning disciples. A type of realized hīnayāna prac-

titioner (arhat) who has achieved the realization of the nonexistence of personal self.
śūnyatā (Tib. *tong pa nyi*) Usually translated as voidness or emptiness. The Buddha taught in the second turning of the wheel of dharma that external phenomena and internal phenomena or the concept of self or "I" have no real existence and therefore are "empty."
three jewels (Tib. *kön chok sum*) These are the Buddha, the dharma, and the sangha.
Thrisong Deutsen (A. D. 790 - 858) Was king of Tibet and invited great Indian saints and yogis to Tibet. He also directed construction of Tibet's first monastery (Samye Ling).
vajrayāna (Tib. *dorje tek pa*) There are three major types of buddhist practices. The hīnayāna, the mahāyanā, and the vajrayāna, which emphasizes the clarity aspect of phenomena and is mainly practiced in Tibet.
wheel of dharma (Skt. *dharmacakra*) The Buddha's teachings correspond to three levels: the hīnayāna, the mahāyāna and the vajrayāna with each set being one turning of the wheel.

Appendix A

Pronuciation	Transliteration	English
bardo	bar do	bardo
'byor ba bcu	'byor ba bcu	10 assets
cha ja chen po	phyag rgya chen po	mahāmudrā
chang chup sem pa	byang chub sems dpa'	bodhisattva
chang chup sem	jang chup sems	bodhicitta
Chenrezig	span ras gzigs	Avalokiteśhvara
chiwa mitakpa	'chi ba mi rtags pa	impermancence
chö	chos	dharma
chö nyi	chos nyid	dharmatā
chö chi khor lo	chos kyi 'khor lo	dharmacakra
dal ba brgyad	dal ba brgyad	8 freedoms
dorje tek pa	rdo rje theg pa	vajrayāna
dra chom pa	dgra bcom pa	arhat
drup chen	grub chen	mahāsiddha
dug	dug	poisons
gen dün	dge 'dun	saṅgha
jor wa chu	'bor ba bcu	10 assets
kor wa	'khor ba	saṃsāra
kor way nye mik	'kor ba'i nyes dmigs	faultsof saṃsāra
kön chok sum	dkon mchog gsum	three jewels
lha ma yin	lha ma yin	jealous god

APPENDIX A TIBETAN TERMS

lam	lam	path
lama	bla ma	guru
lay	las	karma
lo dok namshi	blo ldog rnam bzhi	4 mind-turnings
mi lu rinpoche	mi lus rin po che	pre. human birth
norbu	nor bu	jewel-like
ngöndro	sngon 'gro	preliminaries
nyön thö	nyan thos	śrāvaka
rang sang gye	rang rgyal	prat. buddha
rikdruk	rigs drug gi skye	6 realms of sam.
shakya tubpa	sha kya thub pa	Buddha sakam.
so sor tar pa	so so thar pa	prātimokṣa
tek pa chen po	theg pa chen po	mahāyāna
tek pa chung wa	theg pa dman pa	hīnayāna
tek pa dorje	rdo rje theg pa	vajrayāna
tel wa gye	dal ba brgyud	8 freedoms
tong pa nyi	stong pa nyid	śūnyatā
tün mong gi ngöndro shi	thun mong gi snon 'gro bzhi	4 found.
yidak	yi dvags	hungry ghost

About the Author

Khenpo Thrangu Rinpoche was born in Kham in 1933. At the age of five he was formally recognized by the Sixteenth Karmapa and the previous situ Rinpoche as the incarnation of the great Thrangu tulku. From the ages of seven to sixteen he entered Thrangu monastery and studied reading, writing, grammar, poetry, astrology, memorized ritual texts and completed two preliminary retreats. At the age of sixteen he began the study of the three vehicles of Buddhism under the direction of Khenpo Lodro Rabsel. He also spent time in retreat. At the age of twenty-three and the time of the Chinese military takeover, Rinpoche left Tibet for Rumtek monastery in Sikkim where the Karmapa had his seat in exile. At the age of thirty-five he took the *geshe* examination before 1,500 monks at Buxador monastic refugee camp in Bengal and was awarded the highest degree of Rabjam. On his return to Rumtek he was named Khenpo or main teacher of Rumtek and all other Kagyu monasteries and became abbot of Rumtek monastery and also of the Nalanda Institute for Higher Buddhist studies also at Rumtek. He has been the personal teacher of the four principle Kagyu tulkus: Shamar Rinpoche, Situ Rinpoche, Jamgon Kongtul Rinpoche, and Gyaltsab Rinpoche.

Thrangu Rinpoche has traveled extensively throughout Europe, the Far East and North America. He is the abbot of Gampo Abbey, In Nova Scotia

ABOUT THE AUTHOR

Canada and of Thrangu House in England. In 1984 he spent several months in Tibet where he ordained over one hundred monks and nuns and visited several monasteries. He has also founded his own monastery Thrangu Tashi Choling in Boudhnath near Kathmandu, Nepal; has a retreat center and college at Namo Buddha in the Kathmandu valley; has established his own primary school for the general education of lay children and young monks, has begun building a nunnery in Boudhnath for women to receive their khenpo degree, and has begun building a monastic college in Sarnath, India.

Several of the works by Rinpoche published in English are *Tranquility and Insight* a detailed book on meditation, *Buddha Nature*, the *Uttara Tantra* by this publisher, the *Song of Lodro Thaye*, the *Differentiating Consciousness and Wisdom*, and a series of texts on mahāmudrā meditation. He also has a book in German and one in Spanish.

Anyone wanting information about Thrangu Rinpoche's activities, programs, or other publications can contact the Namo Buddha Seminar, 1390 Kalmia Avenue, Boulder, CO 80304-1813 or by telephone (303) 449-6608.

Index

actions of immediate result 23
animal realm 10, 76-77
appendix of Tibetan words 94-95
attachment 42
Avalokiteshvara mantra 31
bardo 46
bodhicitta 68
Buddha Kāshyapa 27
Buddha Shākyamuni 27-28
Buddha Maitreya 27
cause and effect 77
composites 78
death 41-44
dharma 1
dharmacakra 28
dharmatā 83
dreaming 74
eight freedoms 6, 9-13
eight mental obstacles 20-25
eight obstacles 13
eight unfavorable circumstances 15-20
five poisions 15
four foundations 83
glossary of terms 86-93
god realm 11, 78-79
hell realm 9-19, 73, 75
hīnayāna 28

INDEX

human realm 80
hungry ghost realm 73, 75-76
impermanence 37-50
India 30
jealous god realm 80
kalpa 27
karma 53-57
kleśa 15
mahāmudrā 2
mahāyāna 28
meditation on impermanence 39-48
Namo Buddha Seminar 97
negative actions 74
ngöndro 40, 84
Padmasambhava 30
Padmasambhava's mantra 31
prātimokṣa vows 24
precious human birth 1-33, 82
preliminary practices *see* ngöndro
reincarnation 8
saṃsāra 2, 73, 83
saṅgha 4
śūnyatā 54
six realms of saṃsāra 6
suffering 84-85
ten assets 6, 26-33
ten virtuous actions 57-67
Thrangu Rinpoche 96-97
three jewels 4
Thrisong Detson, king 30
vajrayāna 28

INDEX

human realm 80
hungry ghost realm 73, 75-76
impermanence 37-50
India 30
jealous god realm 80
kalpa 27
karma 53-57
klesa 15
mahamudra 2
mahayana 28
meditation on impermanence 39-48
Namo Buddha Seminar 97
negative actions 74
ngondro 40, 84
Padmasambhava 30
Padmasambhava's mantra 31
pratimoksa vows 24
precious human birth 1-33, 82
preliminary practices see ngondro
reincarnation 8
samsara 2, 73, 83
sangha 4
sunyata 54
six realms of samsara 6
suffering 84-85
ten assets 6, 26-33
ten virtuous actions 57-67
Thrangu Rinpoche 96-97
three jewels 4
Thrisong Detson, king 30
vajrayana 28